THE
MAN
WITH THE
BLACK
VALISE

JOHN GODDARD

THE
MAN
WITH THE
BLACK
VALISE

Tracking the Killer of Jessie Keith

DUNDURN
TORONTO

Publisher: Scott Fraser | Acquiring editor: Kathryn Lane | Editor: Allison Hirst
Designer: Laura Boyle
Cover image: shutterstock.com/Traveller Martin
Printer: Webcom, a division of Marquis Book Printing Inc.

Library and Archives Canada Cataloguing in Publication

Title: The man with the black valise : tracking the killer of Jessie Keith / John Goddard.
Other titles: Tracking the killer of Jessie Keith
Names: Goddard, John, 1950- author.
Description: Includes bibliographical references and index.
Identifiers: Canadiana (print) 20190133473 | Canadiana (ebook) 20190135778 | ISBN 9781459745360
(softcover) | ISBN 9781459745377 (PDF) | ISBN 9781459745384 (EPUB)
Subjects: LCSH: Keith, Jessie, 1880-1894—Death and burial. | LCSH: Chattelle, Almede -1895. | LCSH: Murder—Investigation—Ontario. | LCSH: Murder—Ontario—History—19th century.
Classification: LCC HV6535.C32 O59 2019 | DDC 364.152/309713—dc23

1 2 3 4 5   23 22 21 20 19

We acknowledge the support of the Canada Council for the Arts and the Ontario Arts Council for our publishing program. We also acknowledge the financial support of the Government of Ontario, through the Ontario Book Publishing Tax Credit and Ontario Creates, and the Government of Canada.

Printed and bound in Canada.

VISIT US AT

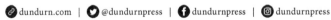
dundurn.com | @dundurnpress | dundurnpress | dundurnpress

Dundurn
3 Church Street, Suite 500
Toronto, Ontario, Canada
M5E 1M2

Contents

Maps

Part One

DEATH
IN THE
SWAMPY
WOOD

CHAPTER 1
Isabella McLeod's Black Valise

FARMERS PARKED THEIR WAGONS outside the exhibition hall to deliver their oversized squashes and pumpkins. Rain fell intermittently. The grassy Ausable River flats glistened under low, luminous clouds. Wives carried in homemade butter, canned peaches, and stuffed birds. The next day was Opening Day of the North Middlesex Agricultural Fair, a harvest celebration that marked one of the year's highlights for the village of Ailsa Craig, a rich farming and cattle centre outside London, Ontario. Only Christmas created more excitement. For the animal competitions, ranchers were preparing their best bulls and heifers. For the poetry recitals, children were rehearsing verses that began, "The Assyrian came down like the wolf on the fold." The only concern was for the racetrack. Rainwater was pooling at the lower turn, creating an expanse of mud that threatened to postpone the horse races, one of the fair's top attractions.

Amédée Chattelle arrived at the fair by chance. He hadn't known about it. He had been heading to northern Michigan to look for logging work but on hearing that prospects were poor had turned around at Sarnia, at the Ontario-U.S. border. From there, he had begun following the Grand Trunk Railway line east toward Toronto, or Ottawa, or maybe Saint-Hyacinthe, Quebec.

Chattelle was a wanderer, a tramp. He had not shaved for several weeks and his greying hair sprouted wildly from his head. His face bore the weathered, dissipated look of homelessness. A low forehead and thick, unexpressive lips lent an impression of dullness, contradicted by a cagey flicker to the eyes. Estimates of his age ranged from thirty-five to fifty. Although of average height, he looked particularly strong and muscular, even among farmers, with a broad back, deep chest, forward-curving shoulders, and thick, meaty hands — hands suggesting "great strength," the newspapers later said. He appeared formidable but exuded an engaging manner. Some quality in him caused people to stop to talk to him and sometimes offer help.

In Ailsa Craig, one such person was Gordon McEwan, a boy of thirteen or fourteen, the son of a moulder at the local Alexander Brothers foundry. "A bright young boy," the newspapers later called him. "An unusually bright lad."

"On October second I met a man near the fairground," McEwan would confidently testify. "I had with me a walking stick which I had made out of the limb of a tree. I had some talk with the man and finally he asked me for the stick and I gave it to him."

The exact date was Tuesday, October 2, 1894. That evening, the rain resumed and Chattelle crossed the fairground to the train station and marshalling yards. He slept overnight in a boxcar, and in the morning another man woke him by climbing noisily into the same carriage. The man didn't look like a tramp, Chattelle said later. He had money and was carrying a bottle of whisky. He gave Chattelle enough change to buy a second bottle, and the two of them started drinking.

"That is where I got drunk," Chattelle said. "While I was drunk I got out of the car and lost the bundle of clothes somewhere. I had a pair of pants that belonged to my suit, and a pair of new suspenders, and undershirt and trousers; I don't know where I hid it; I was tight."

Chattelle never found the extra clothes and never saw the other man again. About noon, he went looking for something to eat. The rain had stopped and the sun was coming out, perfect weather for the fair. He walked through a neighbourhood of large residential lots, many supporting both a house and a small barn for keeping horses and chickens, and perhaps a cow. At a quarter past one, Angus McLean, an engineer at the local Gunn & Co. flax mill, saw the tramp lying on the wet grass next to a walking stick.

"He asked me for a dime," McLean testified. "I told him I thought he was drunk and did not deserve it."

McLean told Chattelle to move on and he rose unsteadily to his feet. Not long afterward, four blocks away, McLean passed him again, standing with the walking stick in front of Donald and Isabella McLeod's house. The engineer continued on his way and the drifter crept unseen around the back.

The McLeods, it turned out, had left home a few minutes earlier to attend the fair. Chattelle broke a window, climbed in, and once he had found something to eat started rifling through a chest of drawers containing Mrs. McLeod's clothes and toiletries. He needed to replace his lost trousers and undershirt, but was drawn instead to the female articles. He was still drunk. He tried on a white petticoat, or woman's underskirt, along with a navy-blue skirt and a black cashmere waistcoat, or vest, trimmed with flowered satin brocade. On his head, he placed a black bonnet and veil, decorated with small black ostrich-feather tips and a row of jet around the rim. In addition, he picked out a brush and comb, several bars of soap, a white apron, an old pair of girl's shoes, a second white petticoat that matched the first one, and a man's black cloth Glengarry cap, or tam-o'-shanter, with a red tassel. He also commandeered a small black suitcase, or valise. Into the bag he put everything he wasn't wearing. On his way out of the house, he left the walking stick next to the cellar door and picked up a green, or possibly blue, umbrella. He later spoke of the break-in this way:

> I went from one house to another and when I came to this house, there was no one in, so I walked in. The woman can't have been long gone. There I dressed myself up in full uniform, right in the house; in the woman's uniform, right out and out, the whole business; took it

from the bureau and walked right out with it, and put my own clothes in the satchel. I had the green umbrella over my head, and my whiskers were longer than they are now. I passed right through the crowd at the Fair.

Young Gordon McEwan spotted him and recognized him from the day before. "I saw him coming from the bush not very far from Mrs. McLeod's house," the boy said. "He was then dressed in women's clothes. He had on a woman's bonnet and veil and a black [navy-blue] skirt. I don't think he had on the waist. He was carrying a valise and a blue umbrella. I had no difficulty in telling who he was, for although he had on women's clothes anybody could see that he was a man. Mr. Fraser also saw him and so did two little girls who were very much frightened by his appearance."

Chattelle climbed a fence onto the railway tracks. He tore the white apron into strips and threw them away, along with the umbrella. Still dressed in Mrs. McLeod's clothes and bonnet, he continued east along the tracks toward Lucan, the next village.

CHAPTER 2
Joseph Hall's Well

EVEN WHEN HE WAS SICK, Joseph Hall could out-dance almost anybody. In June 1888, when he was twenty-four years old and a free spirit, Joseph entered a late-night dance contest against a neighbouring farmer, John Coursey, at a barn on the edge of Lucan. The evening began with a progressive euchre tournament. At midnight, food was served and an Italian string band from nearby London began to play. Afterward came what the *Exeter Times* called "the principal event of the evening," a competition between Hall and Coursey, officiated by a man known to everybody as "Christopher H."

"The four dances were a Highland fling, statue clog, Irish jig and a well known dance in this section, called lean on the Hodgins," the newspaper said. "Mr. Hall was the winner of the three first dances and Mr. Coursey singularly distinguished himself in the latter, his steps being simply a marvel of grace and beauty. The contest lasted one hour and seventeen minutes and at the close Mr. Hall, who was laboring under a severe attack of pneumonia, was completely used up."

Hall was declared the winner but his rival proved a poor sport. As a young woman stepped forward to pin a purple silk rosette on Hall's chest, Coursey demanded a rematch.

"Mr. Coursey contends," the newspaper said, "that if he has on his regulation dancing jump [dance costume] he can defeat Mr. Hall with ease."

Six years later, at the age of thirty, Joseph Hall started to put his life in order and settle down. On September 19, 1894, he married twenty-year-old Eleanor "Ellie" Jell, who was three months pregnant. Presiding at the wedding was the bride's uncle, the Venerable Archdeacon Marsh of neighbouring Oxford County. Hall also purchased some farmland extending east of the Lucan village limits and south of the railway line.

On Thursday, October 4, the day after the harvest fair opened in Ailsa Craig, he encountered Amédée Chattelle. Maybe Hall saw him passing on the tracks, or maybe Chattelle knocked on the farmhouse door to ask for food or work. In any case, Hall hired him to dig a well, and the drifter moved in with the farmer and his expectant wife.

The weather was turning cold. Nighttime temperatures were dipping toward the freezing mark, and the days were getting shorter. "Harsh raw cold morning, first appearance of very slight flurry of snow," Lucan postmaster William Porte wrote in his daybook on Sunday, October 14, ten days after Chattelle's arrival.

That same day, Walker Jell, Ellie's eighteen-year-old brother, dropped by for a Sunday visit with the Halls from nearby Clandeboye. At some point during his stay, Jell noticed a black valise belonging to Chattelle and remembered reading about a recent break-in.

"During one of the afternoons of the Ailsa Craig Fair," the local newspaper had said, "a short, thick-set tramp … broke in to Mr. Donald McLeod's residence and stole a valise and a quantity of Mrs. McLeod's wearing apparel."

Jell became suspicious. He demanded to see the bag, and when he opened it, found a navy-blue skirt, two white petticoats, and numerous other articles of female clothing. He asked Chattelle why he was travelling with women's clothes.

"[Chattelle] became alarmed," the *Toronto Globe* later reported. "He said he was on his way to Toronto from the mines, and the clothes belonged to his wife."

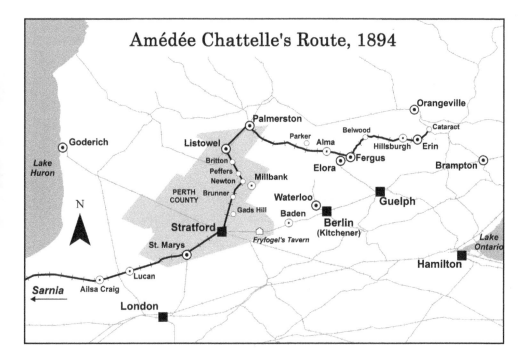

Jell suggested they take a ride into Ailsa Craig to check his story, but somehow, in his engaging way, the drifter managed to lower the tension. He evaded further examination and the next morning said he had to be on his way. The reformed Joseph Hall, anxious to avoid disorder, paid him five dollars for digging the well and said he was free to leave.

The next town was St. Marys, twenty-five kilometres along the rail line. Chattelle arrived there on foot before noon the following day. Residents might have noticed his muscular build, stooped shoulders, and large, powerful hands, but later they mostly recalled his stiff black hat with the wide brim. Where he got it, he never said. Townsfolk referred to it as "a Christy hat," or "a Christy," because it was in a style made by Christy & Co. Ltd., of London, England. Nobody reported seeing a valise. Perhaps, mindful of the confrontation with Jell, the drifter stashed it somewhere by the tracks and retrieved it later.

With the week's wages burning a hole in his pocket, Chattelle went on a shopping spree. At one of the leather stores on Queen Street East, he bought a pair of black, laced shoes with toecaps. Next, he walked into Crozier's Barber Shop, which occupied a wood-frame building at Queen and Water Streets, and ordered a haircut and a shave. The barber, Bertram Teskey, remembered the customer's "squeaky" new shoes. "It's the last shave I'll get this year," Chattelle told Teskey. "I'm going to let it grow after this."

When the barber finished, Chattelle lingered for nearly an hour, and with some of the other customers got into a guessing game about their ages.

"I am seventy-six," one man said.

"And what might I be?" Chattelle said.

Estimates ranged between forty and fifty.

"You're all wrong," Chattelle answered playfully, who was in fact fifty. "I look young for my age. I'm sixty."

On leaving the barbershop, he walked one block east to the A.H. Lofft & Co. clothing and dry-goods store. From the sales clerk, William Rogers, he bought a pair of grey workman's overalls with brown stripes, made from a coarse twill fabric called cottonade. They were to replace the

The clothing and dry-goods store A.H. Lofft & Co., shown in 1905, occupied what is now 139 and 141 Queen Street East in St. Marys. Chattelle bought a pair of grey cottonade overalls there with brown stripes.

trousers he had mislaid while drunk in Ailsa Craig. He paid one dollar and Rogers issued a receipt, which the customer stuffed into his pocket.

Exiting the store, he crossed the street and went directly to Gilpin's Hardware, which occupied the middle unit of a handsome limestone building known as the Guest Block. "A clerk in Mr. J.C. Gilpin's hardware store sold a stranger … an IXL pocket knife, for which he paid 28 cents," the *St. Marys Argus* later reported. The knife would turn out to be his murder weapon. Other newspapers described it as "razor sharp."

The next day was Tuesday, October 16. The drifter took the railway tracks out of town and advanced toward Stratford with his powerful stride. Two incidents that day suggested opposite sides of his character — amiable wanderer and criminal threat.

At twenty minutes to noon, he called at a farmhouse to ask for something to eat. The farmer, William McCaffy, invited him in for "dinner," the noon meal. The men ate together and chatted for an hour. Afterward, Chattelle offered to work in return for the food, but McCaffy said no, he had enjoyed the company. "He wore a Christy hat," the farmer later recalled, "and carried a satchel, which he left outside."

Late that afternoon, on the same road to Stratford, a man walking from the direction of St. Marys and matching Chattelle's description tried to grab a young woman. Whether Chattelle was, in fact, the man would never be confirmed, but when newspapers ran the story several weeks later, they attributed the attempt directly to him.

"It was just dark," the *Stratford Daily Herald* said. "The brute grabbed the young woman, and she in great fright screamed and began to run. Chattelle chased after her and snatched for her again, the woman feeling his hand almost clutch her dress. The young woman still screaming ran into a neighbouring house, but when they came to look for the pursuer he had disappeared."

That evening, Chattelle arrived in Stratford. Between five thirty and six o'clock, Donald Ross, a train-engine driver, answered his back door and gave him something to eat. A short time later, the tramp stole three items, including two articles of women's clothing, from a clothesline belonging to William Maynard, local manager of the Bank of Commerce. Chattelle lifted a towel, a blue waistcoat with white polka dots, and black stockings with the letter *N* embroidered into each with white thread. The *N* stood for *Nora*, the banker's daughter. That night, at the city's northern limits, the thief built a fire against the autumn chill and went to sleep.

The next day was Wednesday, October 17. Nothing eventful happened that day or the next, but witnesses added subtle details to an emerging portrait of the tramp carrying the black valise. Eleven kilometres beyond Stratford, just past Gads Hill, he spoke to Alfred Poole, a railway "section man," so-called because he provided upkeep on a long section of track. Chattelle said he once worked on the railway at Oscoda, in northern Michigan, and he and Poole discovered they knew people in common. Chattelle wore leather harvest mitts, Poole said, and carried a black valise.

That evening, a little farther north, Chattelle called at Reuben York's farmhouse and asked for supper. York's wife objected, but Chattelle pleaded with them. He was hungry. He had spent all his money but offered to pay the couple with his most valuable remaining possessions — what he described as a set of pearl cufflinks and a gold-plated collar button with a pearl backing. The items also held sentimental value for him. They bore a connection to his family and Quebec birthplace.

"Did your wife not refuse to give me my supper?" Chattelle later testified, tacitly confirming the place and time, "And did I not pull those out of my pocket and offer them in payment for my supper, as I had no money, and they cost me $1.30 at my own half-brother's store at Saint-Hyacinthe?"

In exchange for the cufflinks and button, the Yorks served Chattelle supper. Afterward, a neighbour, William Lamb, spotted him on the Yorks' property building a fire, as though settling down for the night. He was wearing overalls with a tear near the top of the right thigh, Lamb later testified. It was the first mention of a tear in the new overalls — a further identifying detail, like the Christy hat and black valise.

On Thursday, October 18, the tramp proceeded toward Listowel. At seven forty-five in the morning, section man John Zimmerman spotted him near Brunner station. At three thirty that afternoon, section man Thomas Glasscock noticed him north of Milverton. At four o'clock, a girl named Addie Tanner handed him something to eat at her family's home one kilometre from Millbank station, also called Newton. At five o'clock, Lena Lather answered the door at her family's farmhouse north of Newton and gave him a piece of bread. He scowled, she said. That evening, between Newton and Peffers, E.O. Flanders, visiting from Wisconsin, watched him light a fire of sticks to warm himself.

A sadder diary entry can scarcely be imagined. On October 19, 1894, William Keith wrote only five words and recorded nothing else in the book for the rest of the year.

On Friday, October 19, the weather turned fair again. The sun turned warm and golden, the sky a deep blue. "Just as fine fall weather as ever was seen in this country," William Porte wrote in his daybook at Lucan.

William Keith, a farmer at the outskirts of Listowel, also kept a log. Typically, he mentioned the weather, what chores he completed, what trips he took into town, and what money he spent and earned. In the previous few days, he had referred to helping a neighbour with threshing. He had detailed selling a dozen ewes and lambs to a trader named Henry Leslie and slaughtering a sheep for the family. His October 19 note was different. On that day, he wrote what must be close to the saddest possible diary entry for a father to write. He managed five words: "This day Jessie was murdered."

CHAPTER 3
A Change of Mood

DESPITE THE BRIGHT WEATHER Chattelle's mood was turning sour. Maybe he was distressed from bartering his cufflinks and collar button, or maybe camping in the open for several nights in a row was taking its toll. In any case, Lena Lather said he scowled when she had given him bread the evening before, the first mention of ill-temper, and several people who saw him the next morning mentioned a similar edginess.

On Friday morning, October 19, between six thirty and seven o'clock, a farmer, John R. Jones, spotted Chattelle walking north along a concession road, one kilometre from the railway line. Suspicions aroused, Jones took a long, hard look. "I could pick him out of a thousand men," he said later.

At eight o'clock, near Peffers, the drifter approached Theresa Loney at her father's farm and asked for something to eat. She gave him breakfast. He wore a stiff hat and overalls with a tear on the side of one leg and left a valise outside. "He had nothing with him at the house, but he had before he came into the house," she said. A little before nine, sisters Emma and Maggie Freeman saw him on their way to school in Peffers. At ten fifteen, Alexander Frame of Stratford passed him at a railway crossing. "Mr. Frame was so close to him that he almost touched him with one of the shafts of the buggy," the *Toronto Globe* said. "The man was mumbling something to himself."

As the tramp continued north toward Britton and Listowel, teenagers Armour Laird and John Attwood were setting out south from Listowel to hunt partridge. At twenty after ten, they passed the Keith farm and saw thirteen-year-old Jessie leave the farmhouse. "Going south towards Stratford on the track, we went first through the bush," Laird later testified, "and saw a partridge but could not get it. Coming back to the track again, we passed the girl just coming out of her own place on the way to town …

"I did not know her to speak to her," the boy said. "We went back into the bush again and further down the track came out just as we heard the 11:30 freight whistle on leaving Britton. Before the freight came along a man came up the track from Stratford way and said, 'Out shooting, eh?'

"I said, 'Yes.'

"'What did you shoot?' he asked.

"'Nothing,' I said.

"'You could not shoot anything, anyway,' he said, quite gruffly. I told him if he would put his hat on a stump I'd show him. Then he went on."

As he listened to Laird's testimony, Chattelle objected to being described as gruff. "I think he is mistaken," the tramp said. "I did not say anything about shooting."

"What *did* you say?" a jury member asked.

"All I did was to pass the time of day with him, the same as I did with the others."

Chattelle proceeded on his way. At five minutes to eleven, he walked north into Britton station, the last station before Listowel. He asked the stationmaster's wife, Sarah Heard, for a drink of water, and she directed him to the water pump. He was carrying a black valise, she said, and "had a hard look to him."

Chattelle quenched his thirst but he was also getting hungry. He had not eaten since eight o'clock that morning. He continued along the tracks and before reaching Listowel left the rail line to approach James Gray's farmhouse. At ten minutes to twelve he knocked on the door and asked the hired girl, Carrie Lentz, for something to eat. When she gave him a piece of bread, he returned down the lane to the road. He wore a stiff black hat and spoke with a French accent, said the girl, one of the only witnesses to mention an accent. Armour Laird also remarked on it later.

Afterward, Thomas Johnston, one of Gray's hired men, saw the tramp leave the farm walking west along the road to rejoin the train tracks, while eating the bread Lentz had given him. A few minutes later, Robert Morris, a drayman, or teamster, saw the man reach the rail line, leading northwest across the front corner of William Keith's farm on the route into town. As Morris continued by horse and buggy, he heard the noon factory whistle blow.

CHAPTER 4
The Swampy Wood

JESSIE KEITH LEFT HER FARMHOUSE that morning at twenty after ten. She set out on foot for Listowel, taking the family's usual shortcut along the tracks, two kilometres straight into town. She was thirteen years old, or "thirteen years, ten months," the newspapers later said. She was also a bright, intelligent child her father said, an assiduous pupil who a year and a half earlier had precociously passed her high-school entrance exam. Instead of continuing her studies, however, she had chosen to stay home to help her mother and made almost daily trips into town on errands.

That day she was wearing her usual going-to-town clothes. She wore a red dress, a navy-blue jacket with two large buttons at the throat, a white silk scarf with red flowers, and a black felt sailor's hat with a bow to one side and two bands of velvet around the crown. She also wore black gloves, black stockings, and good shoes with laces. She carried a small purse with almost exactly enough money to buy what she needed. Townsfolk knew her for her sweet, angelic face, and the long dark-brown hair that trailed down her back in a single, thick braid.

At the post office, Jessie picked up the *Listowel Banner* and the *Toronto Globe* for her father, and at the dry-goods store purchased a package of

It is hereby Certified

That _Jessie Keith_

has passed the ENTRANCE EXAMINATION required by the Education Department for admission to a Collegiate Institute or High School.

Dated at _Listowel_

31st July 1893

Wm. Alexander
Inspector of Public Schools.

FORM 175.

The Keith family preserved the certificate showing that Jessie passed her high-school entrance exam when she was twelve years old. Instead of continuing her studies, she elected to help her mother on the farm.

pot barley for her mother. As she started home, she ran into a former school friend, Edith Lephardt, and the two girls walked together down Mill Street, now Wallace Avenue South. They parted at the rail crossing and Jessie continued out of town alone.

Three railway maintenance workers, or section men, passed her shortly afterward. They were travelling into town in a handcar for the noon meal. They knew the girl by sight, having seen her often, but didn't speak to her. After eating, they got back on the handcar, and at almost the exact spot where they had been working before dinner, found newspapers and a torn parcel of pot barley scattered on the tracks. The papers bore the address of the Keith farm, and section boss Richard Stanton hurried to alert the family.

"I was ploughing in the field after the noon hour when Stanton, the section man on the railway, came down carrying the papers and some barley that he had found on the track," Jessie's father, William Keith,

"Highly regarded by his neighbours and the citizens of the town of Listowel," the *Atwood Bee* said of William Keith, Jessie's father. The photo is undated. At the time of the girl's death he was fifty-five years old.

later said. "'Is your girl home?' [Stanton] asked, and I said, 'No.' 'Then,' he said, 'something must have happened to her, [because] I found these things with your name on them.'"

Keith remembered the time as twenty after one. Jessie had been expected home an hour earlier. He tied his plough horses to the fence, and with Stanton walked up the tracks to where the other section men, Samuel Strain and Richard Forbes, were waiting. The distance wasn't far. Farms at the time were divided into narrow strips, and the newspapers and barley were found two fields over, at the top of a slight rise. At that spot, Jessie would have been walking in plain sight of the road and within view of almost every public building in town. Jessie's mother later remembered glancing out the dining-room window while putting dinner on the table and catching the flash of a red dress in the distance. "Jessie's coming," she said, but when the girl didn't arrive shortly afterward, the family started without her. Mrs. Keith later realized that she had not glimpsed Jessie walking on the tracks but being hauled over the fence into the east field.

William Keith and the section men began to search the area. In the grass next to the spilled barley they found two patches of blood and on the east fence more blood. On the other side of the fence, they spotted two sets of footprints, one set larger than the other, leading one hundred metres across a freshly ploughed field into a swampy wood. For part of the way, the heels of the smaller prints appeared to be dug into the ground, as though to resist being forced along. At other places, the prints dissolved into drag marks. The searchers entered the bush, thick with undergrowth, and after nearly an hour and a half, at about three o'clock, Samuel Strain stepped on something soft and saw two bare feet spring from the undergrowth.

It was Jessie. She lay flat on her back completely covered with moss and rotten wood stripped from nearby tree trunks and fallen logs. One newspaper described the surroundings as "picturesque": A young maple tree grew near where the girl's head rested. Three or four crumbling oak trees lay at her feet and on either side of her body. Overhanging the entire scene stretched "a healthy young cedar, the branches of which formed a canopy for the natural coffin," the report said. The site evoked the English folk tale "Babes in the Wood," the account said, in which two small children are left to die in the forest and a robin covers them in strawberry leaves.

But this was no fairytale. On brushing away part of the covering, the men discovered almost unimaginable gore. The body was nude and the throat slit — "from ear to ear," the newspapers said. Around the throat was wrapped a white petticoat, soaked crimson with blood. The hair was matted with blood, the nose was bloodied, and purple bumps rose from the forehead. Under the lower lip could be seen what looked like a deep knife wound, as though the girl had ducked to avoid an initial stab to the throat. The lower torso was mutilated and some body parts were missing. The clothes were also missing, although not far away Charles Gowing, a passing hunter who had joined the search, found a white silk scarf with red flowers, soaked with blood. A full understanding of what had happened would come only later, but the searchers instantly grasped the enormity of the crime. The innocence of the victim, the barbarity of the act, in broad daylight on a Friday noon hour, almost within sight of the girl's home — the killing stands as one of the most savage in Canadian history.

"The most revolting crime ever perpetuated in Canada, if not on this continent," the *Listowel Standard* called it.

"Hanging is too easy for such a black-hearted monster," the *Atwood Bee* said. "The details of the murder are so revolting in their cruelty, that it is difficult to believe that such a fiend could have existed in this fair province."

In fact, many people refused to believe it. They turned to the only explanation, however implausible, that they could think of, which was that Jack the Ripper must be loose in rural Ontario. The unidentified serial killer, who six years earlier, in 1888, had butchered five prostitutes late at night in the Whitechapel District of London, England, must have emigrated to Perth County to kill an innocent farm girl at midday in the open countryside.

"The 'Jack the Ripper' theory is quite popular here," the *Perth Courier* reported three days after the killing, "and all the literature of the Whitechapel murders obtainable has been eagerly scanned for particulars to support the idea."

Within hours of the body's discovery, at seven fifteen that evening, law-enforcement officials and news reporters boarded a train at Stratford for the trip north to the crime scene. The party included Perth County Crown attorney John Idington, Perth County sheriff John Hossie, and Dr. James Rankin, the coroner. At eight twenty, in the darkness, the train stopped at the rise in the field to let them off. A knot of twenty men stood waiting beside the tracks, among them William Keith. "He carried a lantern, which dimly showed his long grey beard and sorrow-clouded face," the *Stratford Evening Beacon* said.

Together, the entire group climbed the east split-rail fence, crossed the freshly ploughed field, and tramped through the swampy wood until they came to the body, now covered with a white sheet. Charles Gowing, the hunter who had found the scarf, sat with his back against a tree and a rifle across his lap. He had been guarding the site all afternoon and evening. Surrounding him among the trees and bushes, partly illuminated by flickering lanterns, stood another two hundred men. The assembly parted for the officials, but when Dr. Rankin leaned over to pull back the sheet, the men surged forward again or scrambled up overlooking trees. "The curiosity displayed by some in their anxiety to get a view of the sickening sight was shockingly indecent," the *Stratford Evening Herald* reported. "The majority," the *Toronto Mail* said more kindly, "[showed a] deep-rooted desire of ascertaining sufficient particulars upon which they could set to work to avenge the crime."

At first, the petticoat around the girl's throat was assumed to be her own, but a closer inspection proved otherwise. It was too big — thirty-two inches around the waist. Jessie's waistline was twenty-seven.

Afterward, the officials surveyed the area. Even in the dark, they found evidence of three separate struggles. At the railway tracks, where the newspapers and barley had been scattered, they identified two splotches of blood. At a point just inside the bush, where Gowing had recovered the bloodied scarf, they could see disturbances to the ground. Deeper into the woods, the scene of the actual slaying, they found the ground badly torn across a two-metre radius, the undergrowth spattered with blood, and a large pool of blood where Jessie must have fallen and died. From there, the killer had evidently moved the body deeper into the bush and covered it with moss, leaves, and rotten wood.

Dr. Rankin immediately ordered an inquest, a type of pretrial hearing required after an untimely death. From the gathering, he selected fifteen men to form a jury, and asked for volunteers to carry the body out of the woods on a stretcher. At the Keith farmhouse, already crowded with neighbours and extended family members, the men laid the body — still covered by the sheet — on a table in the parlour. With the jury present, Rankin and Idington took three witness statements. Charles Gowing told of finding the scarf. William Keith described the search with the section men. Jane Keith, his wife and the mother of the girl, itemized the clothes Jessie had worn to town. The scarf had been fastened in such a way as to not fall off easily, she said, suggesting the attack must have been ferocious. After taking the statements Coroner Rankin adjourned the inquest. It was to be resumed, he said, in exactly one week at Listowel Town Hall.

Two Listowel physicians arrived. At one o'clock in the morning, doctors Samuel Rutherford and George Watson began a post-mortem that continued for four hours. Jack the Ripper could not have killed the girl, Dr. Rutherford would later say. During the Whitechapel murders he had happened to be visiting London. There, the butchery had been carried

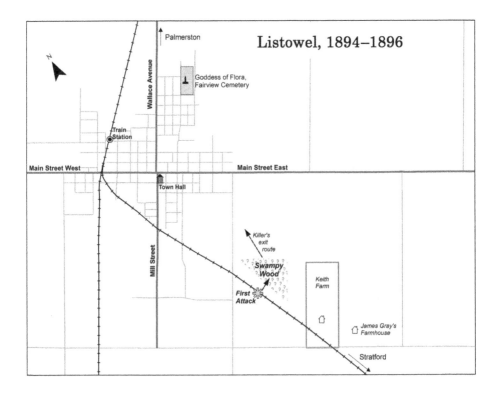

Jessie Keith stands proudly in the front row, sixth from the right, with fellow pupils at Brock's School in 1891, when she was ten years old, a darling girl. Her brother, Sandy, in the only known surviving picture of him, also appears in the front row, third from the left, hands in front of him. Photo damage partly shades his face. The rare image was collected in a scrapbook by the Listowel Women's Institute.

out with "rough skill," he said. In the swampy wood, he said, "the hacking was as if done by a madman."

William Keith appeared more stunned by events than shattered. He was fifty-five years old, an energetic man in the peak of health, with a full head of close-cropped hair and a birds-nest beard shorn several inches below his chin. "One of the best citizens of the county," the *Atwood Bee* called him. "[He] is most highly regarded by his neighbours and the citizens of the town of Listowel." At the age of fifteen, he had immigrated to Canada from Aberdeenshire, Scotland, and had lived in the area for thirty-nine years. The family had lived at their present location for twelve years. Keith ran a dairy herd, grew crops, and served as founding head of the North Perth Farmers' Institute. Jane Keith, whose maiden name was McGeorge, originated from nearby Grey County, north of Listowel. She was forty-one years old. The couple had two other children, sixteen-year-old Ida and nine-year-old Alexander, or "Sandy." William's unmarried younger brother, Alexander, also lived with the family.

"I hardly realize yet what has happened," William Keith told the *Toronto Globe* in his broad, Scottish accent. "They are not bothering me about theories, but the calculation is that she was struck on the head while walking along the track and stunned. Then her body was dragged through the field into the woods, she was first outraged [raped] and then nearly cut to pieces."

CHAPTER 5
Suspicion Focuses on One Man

LISTOWEL PRIDED ITSELF as "the town of stately homes." Entrepreneurs, lawyers, and local politicians typically built houses to suit their individual taste and style. If one chose a Georgian pattern, another might pick a Queen Anne or Italianate design. Some residences featured columns and towers, others porches and gables, still others marble fireplaces and stained-glass windows, each owner vying to outdo his neighbour in embellishment and flair.

Behind only Stratford, Listowel ranked as Perth County's number two manufacturing town. With a population of two thousand, it functioned as a small but prosperous farming and industrial centre. Its top business was piano-making. In 1892, three local visionaries founded Morris, Feild, Rogers Company Limited, later renamed Morris Pianos, employing one hundred workers in a four-storey building of local white brick. The firm shipped pianos as far away as Britain, France, Germany, Spain, and South Africa.

In 1891, a local tannery expanded to become part of the Breithaupt Leather Company, one of the country's largest leather firms, based in what is now Kitchener. Beginning in the 1870s, "flax king" John Livingston directed a regional operation as part of the J. & J. Livingston Linseed

Oil Company, the largest flax enterprise in North America. The Bamford brothers operated planing mills that produced building materials. Partners Gilles and Martin manufactured farm machinery. B.F. Brook ran a woolen mill. John Watson founded a brewery. Robert T. Kemp established a marble works, producing, among other items, polished tombstones.

Listowel's streets were graded and its sidewalks levelled. Its shade trees were on their way to lush maturity, offering protection and comfort from the midday sun. By any measure, the town lived up to its reputation as a safe, salubrious community in which to thrive and raise a family. On Friday, October 19, 1894, however, the town's sense of order and stability was shattered.

By the next morning, the men who had viewed the body in the swampy wood had also spread the word. Local news reporters had filed their first bulletins, and Toronto editors had dispatched staff correspondents to Listowel on the earliest trains. Emotions were running high.

"To say that the town is stirred up ... feebly expresses the situation," the *Toronto Mail* reported Saturday on page one. The story continued:

> Never before has anything happened in this peaceful community that in any way approaches the marvelous brutality of the deed, and all over the town, in every private and public house, on every farm and concession line, where the matter is known, knots of people are assembled, excitedly discussing the details. Business is almost temporarily suspended, so engrossing is the topic. Many people who have heretofore been characterized as eminently law-abiding, who have never been known to even hurt a cat, have boldly declared that they would not hesitate to lynch the human fiend who committed the deed if they could find him. The topic, like a great national calamity, has dispelled formality and ceremony of any kind between citizens and strangers, and everyone talks about the matter with the first man they meet, having a common interest in bringing to justice the perpetrator.

From the start, suspicion focused on one man. On the day of the murder, several witnesses reported having seen a tramp in the vicinity. Teenagers Armour Laird and John Attwood, the partridge hunters, told police about meeting a stout, weather-beaten man with a French accent south of Britton station. Listowel mayor Featherstone Smith, who had been riding with T.F. Foley, a Massey-Harris farm machine agent from Stratford, reported seeing a man of rough appearance at a crossing close to Britton station. Carrie Lentz, the servant girl at Gray's farm, spoke of giving a ruddy-faced drifter a piece of bread. A farmer named Johnston Kidd, who had been tilling a field beyond the swampy wood on Friday afternoon, said he had called "good day" to a heavy-looking stranger. When the man asked for a drink of water, Kidd said, he directed him to the pump in the yard next door. The neighbour, Jane Ann Cattell, said she watched the tramp at the pump from her window. Henry Leslie, a cattle and sheep buyer, and his wife, Sarah, recounted having been travelling by buggy outside Listowel and passing a thickset, weather-beaten man with a hard look.

From Stratford, Crown Attorney Idington issued a public bulletin. "Murder!" it began. "On Friday, 19th October, 1894, Jessie Keith of Elma township, near Listowel, was foully murdered by a supposed tramp, about twelve o'clock, noon. The public are hereby warned to be on the lookout for any tramp or suspicious stranger."

Idington described the suspect as stout, five feet, nine inches tall, 190 to 200 pounds, and about thirty-five years old. He had a heavy body, short neck, full chest, slightly stooped shoulders, dark complexion, and a hard look to the eyes. He was wearing a rusty black coat, a stiff black Christy hat with a brim, pants lighter than the coat, and black laced shoes with toecaps.

The bulletin emphasized one further detail. Some witnesses recalled seeing the suspect carrying a small black satchel. Police were seeking, the newspapers said, "a man with a black valise."

CHAPTER 6
The Burial

ON SUNDAY, TWO DAYS AFTER THE KILLING, William and Jane Keith buried their daughter. The weather proved bright and warm, a perfect autumn day.

Ever since the news broke, friends and acquaintances had been arriving at the farmhouse, offering condolences and placing wreaths in the parlour, where the body lay. By Sunday morning, hundreds of farmers and village folk from as far away as Mitchell, Wingham, Palmerston, Elmira, and Stratford were also converging on the farm.

"All day long, crowds of people, some of them from a considerable distance, visited the house and then crossed through the fields to the [railway] track and from there to the scene of the crime," the *Stratford Beacon* reported. "The first indication of the crime was the pot barley that had been spilled on the track ... but there was not a grain of it left yesterday afternoon. Men and women picked it up with diligent industry, selecting it carefully, grain by grain from the sand, and carried it off to keep as a memento of the innocent young girl who had lost her life in such a horrible way. Then, the little maple and cedar saplings growing around

Curiosity-seekers stand in the swampy wood where Jessie's body was discovered, her head lying near the maple sapling marked by the white cloth or paper. On the morning of the burial, crowds picked the railway tracks clean of pot barley and rifled the murder scene for branches to make into walking sticks.

the several points of interest in the woods were cut off and whittled into walking sticks by the hundred."

There was to be no church service. There were to be no Christian prayers. William and Jane Keith counted themselves as secularists, or freethinkers, members of a movement that rejected religious orthodoxy and embraced human reason as a guide to ethical living. Their children had never attended Sunday school, and later in the day William Keith would feel obliged to refute a malicious suggestion that Jessie had joined a Methodist congregation. A "large number" of clergymen had offered to conduct a Christian funeral, Keith said. He told them he appreciated their sympathy but at the same time had implored local secularist leader William Hay, a miller and one of Listowel's preeminent citizens, to oversee

Secularist leader William Hay officiated at Jessie's interment, urging the extraordinarily large crowd to express their grief to the family through "kindly words and acts." At the graveside, he ordered Rev. Frederick Gunner to hold his tongue.

the interment. At first Hay had declined. He disliked the spotlight and had recommended Congregational Church pastor Robert Hopkins for the job, but the Keiths had insisted. They did not want a Christian burial. They wanted a secular one.

The cortège to the cemetery was scheduled for two o'clock. As the hour drew near, mourners assembled in the expansive fields behind the Keith house. "Never has such a sight been seen in the county, seldom probably in the history of any rural constituency," the *Toronto Mail* said. "The fields," said the *Toronto Globe*, "looked like a crowded fair ground." Some people stood with their freshly cut walking sticks, others next to their bicycles. Surrounding everyone were horse-drawn buggies, carriages, wagons, and carts.

"Fully five hundred conveyances were gathered in the ten-acre field in which the Keith house stands," the *Stratford Herald* said. "The field was almost completely filled, and for a quarter of a mile either way on the road in front of his place the fence was lined with carriages."

At one point, six young pallbearers emerged from the farmhouse and laid the casket on a table, allowing people to file past and view the girl, the body covered but the face exposed. The casket bore the inscription, JESSIE M. KEITH, DIED OCTOBER 19, 1894: AGED 13 YEARS 10 MONTHS.

"As they gazed on the sweet face, disfigured with cuts and bruises," the *Stratford Beacon* said, "it was no wonder that women who were total strangers cried bitterly and that strong men shuddered."

At the last moment, George Watson, one of the physicians who had conducted the autopsy, agreed to remove the girl's eyes. He did not want to do it, he later wrote to the *Globe*. "The multitude," he said, demanded that he preserve the retinas, superstitiously believing that they retained the image of the last thing the girl saw — her killer. The retinas could be photographed, the photographs enlarged, and the killer identified, people in the crowd insisted. "I distinctly stated the impossibility of such a process," the physician wrote in response to later criticism, "but the parties desiring it tried were so numerous and urgent … that I consented."

As Dr. Watson, in private, began the final mutilation, secularist leader Hay climbed onto a rig behind the farmhouse to address the throng. He said nothing about secularism. Rather, he summed up what had happened in the swampy wood, read Crown Attorney Idington's description of the suspect, chronicled what was known of the tramp's movements, and encouraged everybody returning home on an easterly or north-easterly

A portrait of Jessie Keith shows her at the age of eight, with an almost angelic face. "Total strangers cried bitterly," said the *Stratford Beacon*.

route after the burial to be on special alert. The suspect appeared to be travelling in that direction, he said. Perhaps sensing the religious backlash that was about to unfold, Hay also urged everybody to show kindness to the family and to each other.

"The occasion was one for showing the brotherhood of man," the *Atwood Bee* paraphrased Hay as saying. "They should bear one another's burdens and by kindly words and acts show that they felt for the family in their grief."

At about two thirty, after the delay with the eyes, the pallbearers hoisted the casket onto a horse-drawn hearse to begin the procession to Fairview Cemetery, at Listowel's north end. In the lead vehicles, Jessie's elder sister, Ida, and younger brother, Sandy, could be spotted. Other family members included William Keith's three brothers — Alexander, James, and George. Jane Keith's father, Samuel McGeorge, was also there along with Jane's brothers, John, Samuel Jr., and Alexander. So many vehicles fell in behind the hearse that the line stretched for nearly three kilometres, meaning that as the last buggy was leaving the Keith farm, the grieving family was already passing through the centre of town. By then, more than half the rigs had deserted the procession to sprint up side streets in the hope of securing the best parking spots at the cemetery and the best standing places at the grave. Spectators also lined the streets.

"A great crowd assembled [along the main route] and every point of vantage was occupied," the *Toronto Mail* reported. "At the cemetery the throng was equally dense, and it was with difficulty that the hearse could be forced through to the open grave."

As the hearse passed through the cemetery gates, a striking figure with white hair fell into step in front of it. "A venerable old man," the *Globe* called him, "who might have stepped out of one of Nathaniel Hawthorn's stories of the Puritan pastors of New England." He was Rev. Frederick Gunner, a retired Congregational minister. He had been one of the clergymen to approach William Keith about conducting a Christian service and been turned down. Now he wasn't about to take "no" for an answer. He walked holding aloft an open prayer book and reading from it aloud, tactlessly including the line, "Naked came I out of my mother's womb, and naked shall I return."

Perhaps because they were walking behind, nobody in the official party heard him. When Hay saw Gunner positioned at the foot of the grave, however, the secularist leader ordered the preacher to stand back.

"I will just stand here," Gunner said, refusing to move.

The pallbearers lowered the coffin into the ground. The first shovelful of earth was tossed. William and Jane Keith bore the moment stoically. William told a friend afterward that sometimes he was not quite sure whether his daughter was dead or alive. He felt as though he were

MRS. KEITH.

A newspaper sketch shows Jane Keith, forty-one years old at the time of her daughter's murder, wearing a veil and mourning clothes. No photograph of her survives.

wandering through a terrible dream, he said, from which he expected to wake. "Mrs. Keith," the *Stratford Beacon* said, "has borne up so well that there is grave fear of a collapse when the intense excitement passes over."

Hay again thanked the assembly for their attendance and sympathy, and everything seemed to be going as well as could be expected when Gunner shouted, "Oh, Lord, grant salvation to these people."

"You just hold your tongue now," Hay said, as the *Herald* reported the exchange.

"I won't," Gunner replied, "and you can't make me."

"If you don't, I will have you arrested."

"I don't think you can have me arrested."

"We will see about that," Hay said emphatically, "and I don't want any more words from you."

Gunner later said that Hay hit him, but Hay denied it, saying he reached over to place a hand over Gunner's mouth. In any case, Gunner fell silent, but once the grave was filled he turned and strode purposefully away. Outside the gates, he mounted a buggy as though ascending a pulpit and, as a crowd gathered around him, launched into one of the most tasteless rants imaginable. For twenty minutes, with supporters egging him on, the preacher berated secularists. He denounced Hay as having manipulated the Keiths into a secular burial, and at one point seemed to lump the Keith family in with the killer — "all infidels," he called them.

"How can I hold my tongue?" the preacher bellowed in one final violation of the innocent girl. "Are Christian ministers to hold their peace and have infidels ride over them…? Should their cemeteries be desecrated by infidels, and the Christian minister be put out? Who rules the universe — God or the wicked? Who did the deed we lament today? Infidels. (Cries of 'Yes.') The man who has done this deed, no matter who he is, is an infidel. He cannot be a Christian. (Cries of 'No.') And now we have seen a dear girl, once a professing Christian and an attendant at a Methodist church, savagely murdered and buried like a dog."

CHAPTER 7
A Star-Crossed Life

BIRTH RECORDS KEPT by the Roman Catholic Church in Saint-Hyacinthe, Quebec, confirm that Amédée Chattelle was born there on February 10, 1844. He was the first child of Jeremiah Chattelle and his second wife, who died when Amédée was four years old. When he was six, his father married for the third time, this time to a widow with seven children of her own. Amédée instantly disliked her. Or, as he put it, "The day he brought his third wife into the house, I stood beside her and looked here [*sic*] in the eyes and told my father I didn't want here [*sic*] in the house; that I could see the devilment in her eyes, and that if she stayed there, I wouldn't."

The information comes from an account Chattelle gave of his life, four months after Jessie Keith's death. The essay wasn't made public at the time. William Keith somehow gained possession of it and suppressed it, then secretly passed it down through the family. It eventually reached Marshall Keith, Jessie's first cousin once removed, the grandson of William Keith's elder brother, James.

In 1967, Marshall showed the document to Cy Bamford, a *Listowel Banner* reporter with a special interest in the case. The Bamford family had always maintained that Cy's grandmother, who had lived in the last house before the railway tracks on Mill Street, gave Jessie a glass of water before her final walk out of town. Family lore makes no mention of Jessie's friend, Edith Lephardt. Instead, it relates that Grandma Bamford "was the last person — with the exception of the murderer — to have talked with the victim and possibly the last to have seen her alive."

On August 10, 1967, the *Banner* published Chattelle's essay for the first time. The original was written in longhand on paper now yellowed with age, Cy Bamford said in an introduction. Chattelle apparently recounted his story to an official, who wrote it down. One page was missing, however; a section that coincided with the time of the murder. The remaining transcript ran to thirty-five hundred words, equivalent to twelve typed legal-size pages, double-spaced.

In the document Chattelle recounts a cruel and loveless childhood. He grew up not knowing his birth mother's name, he says, a chilling admission, and chronicles a lifetime of wanderings to places as far-flung as Egypt, India, and the Caribbean. A preciseness of detail lends authenticity to his story, but the account also sounds sanitized, self-serving, and untrustworthy. It never mentions any serious brushes with the law.

Chattelle's father, Jeremiah, had children from his first two wives and with the third marriage seven more, the transcript says, but the families blended poorly. One day, Amédée was arguing with a stepbrother his own age. The third wife sided with her birth son, Jeremiah sided with his wife, and Amédée got a whipping. Such injustices were common. Sometimes the boy ran across the street to the home of an aunt, the wife of his father's brother, and she protected him. At other times he disappeared for two or three days. When he was nine he escaped to a half-sister's house on the St. Lawrence River, but she sent him home and his father gave him another whipping.

"Then I ran away and went off into the country," Chattelle says in the essay. He was eleven years old. On crossing the St. Lawrence River to Montreal, he met a steamboat captain, who gave him a basket with a number on it. The number allowed him to work "at the market," likely Bonsecours Market — built in the late 1840s at the city's port and Montreal's principal public market for more than a hundred years.

Within a few days, he met a wealthy woman who wished "to keep me in place of her dead boy," he says. He stayed with her for eight or nine months. Afterward, he started back toward his birthplace, stopping at a town transliterated in the document as "Saint Amos," but likely Saint-Damase, fifteen kilometres short of Saint-Hyacinthe. "I found a home there with a farmer and I stayed with him 11 months, and that is where I made my first Communion," he says.

A slightly different version of the episode appeared in the *Toronto Globe* at the time of the murder. "On his way home he was overtaken by an illness at [Saint-Damase] which compelled him to call a halt," the paper said, without giving a source. "He was taken in by a kind-hearted family, who not only nursed him through his illness but took a decided interest in him after his recovery and showed it by preparing him for his first communion."

One Sunday, Jeremiah showed up. How he discovered his son's whereabouts, Chattelle doesn't say, only that his father demanded that he return home with him. Chattelle told his father that he liked living with the farmer better than with his own family, but his father reclaimed the boy anyway.

"When I came home with my bundle under my arm, my stepmother wanted to know if I came to stay," the memoir reads. "I said 'Yes.' She said I should stay where I was, my father had enough to do without feeding my stinking mouth."

And so Chattelle's permanent wanderings began. The boy took off again, and after living two or three months with various relatives, struck out on his own. How old he might have been he doesn't say, but it is possible to calculate. He says he spent the next two years in Nova Scotia driving oxen to haul timber, three years in Vermont working for a farmer, and three years fighting in the American Civil War on the Union side in Virginia, principally in the Battles of Gettysburg (1863), Weldon Railroad (1864), and Cedar Creek (1864). In the summer of 1865, he says, he visited his father for three days in Saint-Hyacinthe. If he was born in 1844, he would have been twenty-one years old at the time of the visit. Putting the other dates together, he would have been absent for eight years, meaning he had left home at thirteen — the same age as Jessie when she died.

Over the next three decades, Chattelle wandered the United States and the world. Sometimes he took physically demanding jobs. He worked at a nail factory in Vermont, laid railway track in New York, built corn cribs in what is now Oklahoma, picked grapes in California, sawed wood in Arkansas, threshed millet seed in Texas, and ran a water pump at an iron mine in northern Michigan.

In the transcript, he often states precisely where he was, who he was with, and what he was doing.

"I boarded with an Irish family of the name of O'Neill," he says of one stay.

"I used to trade with a man named Zugerman there, a grocer," he says of another.

"I started to go to Texas," he says of yet another, "and I met on my way a young fellow from Rochester, N.Y., Jake Kelter, we journed [*sic*] along till we got to Dennison, Texas."

He recalls his exact wages.

"I went to Spokane Falls where I worked by the day carpentering at $4.50 a day," he says of one job.

"I fed cattle all winter at $35.00 a month with board for a man named Spears," he says of another.

Although perpetually restless, he also appears competent and resourceful.

"I helped clear the right of way for the town, and made a road for them to haul their ore and charcoal," he says of other work he performed at the Michigan iron mine. "I was boss over 25 or 30 men all the time. I stayed three years."

Chattelle twice mentions jail, but never violent crime. "I put in three months in Milwalkee [*sic*] on a charge of vagrancy," he says of one occasion. Another time, in Maine, he called at a minister's house to ask to stay the night. When he found nobody home, he crawled through a window and went to bed. In the morning the minister found him and called the police. What happened next speaks to Chattelle's cleverness and perhaps his sense of humour.

"[The jailer] was about five times as strong as me," the memoir reads, "he could handle me like a child, but I told him several times I could get away from him, and he always laughed at me. That night I got an opportunity and locked him in the cell himself and went away. I was jailer for a little while that night."

Sometimes Chattelle went to sea. Beginning in his early twenties, he sailed on various merchant ships out of Providence, Rhode Island, and after two years voyaged between Bangor, Maine, and the West Indies. Soon he was crossing the Atlantic Ocean to London and Liverpool, then to India and Australia. On his return, he jumped ship in Boston, but years later took to the sea again, once enjoying a layover in Egypt and Arabia.

"While [the schooner] stayed at Alexandria, a lot of us went ashore and rambled in the country for six weeks in the desert," he says. "Fourteen miles south of Alexandria there is a pillar, put up by Pontious [*sic*] Pilate [likely meaning Pompey's Pillar, a Roman triumphal column], two stones on top of one another, each 75 feet high; the base of the foundation is three steps high of solid granite. At the foot of it are lots of petrified bodies. We crossed the Nile and went East till we got opposite Mount Zion, and on over Mount Carmel, and onto the River Jordan: we came to [the Biblical site of] Gilgal: that is as far as we went."

In March 1894, after further voyages and wanderings, Chattelle says he "tramped" all the way to Saint-Hyacinthe from California. He arrived in June — four months before the killing. All he says about the visit is, "I worked on a dam below St. Hyacinth [*sic*] till September, when I quit and came up here [to Ontario]."

The *Globe* fleshes out this part of the story, having sent a reporter to Saint-Hyacinthe after the murder. By the time Chattelle returned to his birthplace, his father and stepmother were dead. The family home had been sold. One of several half-brothers, Eusebe, offspring of the third wife, ran a store that carried groceries and knick-knacks. Another half-brother sold shoes and a third was in jail. Two sisters lived as nuns in a convent. Almost immediately on his arrival, Chattelle landed a job nine kilometres downriver with the Electric Light Company.

"Chattelle was employed here about two months as a laborer," his foreman, a Mr. Lefebvre, told the *Globe*. "I considered him a first-class workman. He attended to his business, never had any quarrel of any kind with the other men, did not talk much about his travels, and I never heard him tell any stories about women."

One Saturday night in September, after the light company paid him, Chattelle quit without notice. As suddenly as he had arrived, he disappeared. He heard there was logging work in northern Michigan, he says, taking him into Ontario for the first time in his life. At the U.S. border at Sarnia, he heard that prospects in Michigan were not good after all and he turned back.

CHAPTER 8
Manhunt

IN THE DAYS FOLLOWING THE MURDER, tramps throughout southwestern Ontario came under special scrutiny. No stranger escaped notice. Near Stratford, police raided a barn at three in the morning, found fourteen vagrants, and detained five of them at the county jail. In Parkhill, nearly a hundred kilometres southwest of Listowel, police locked up a man who fit the suspect's physical description but wore different clothes. At St. Clements, forty kilometres southeast of Listowel, police arrested a man then released him after questioning. In Listowel itself, two itinerant men were arrested and released, only to be arrested and released again in Atwood. In the Niagara village of Stevensville, police picked up a suspicious character. He gave his name as Simpson, said he had been working in Buffalo and was heading to London where he had friends, but seemed to know little about Buffalo or London. As far away as Omemee, nearly a hundred kilometres northeast of Toronto, a posse of a dozen citizens arrested a suspect and police locked him up. In Pickering, thirty kilometres east of Toronto, police arrested a tramp with blood on his coat, which he said came from a fight in Toronto. At Alma, thirty-five kilometres east of Listowel, police arrested a man closely matching the police description, but he turned out to be James McCabe, a retired schoolteacher who liked to roam the district visiting friends and relatives.

Some efforts to apprehend the killer proved almost comical. Outside Listowel, a farm-implements agent on his way to a rural auction spotted a man crossing a field. The agent, armed with a revolver, jumped out of his buggy and gave chase. The suspect disappeared into the woods. The agent proceeded to the neighbouring farm where the sale was taking place and, with the auctioneer and others, organized a search. It ended when one of the pursuers realized he was the man they were looking for. He had taken a shortcut through the woods to attend the sale.

At one point, word came of an arrest at Moorefield, twenty-four kilometres east by road. Two police officers with a fast team of horses were said to be delivering a man identified as George McKay. The officers described him as thirty-four years old, well built, of medium height, and dressed in a dark suit of clothes. In Listowel, a mob of five hundred people assembled to meet the coach.

"It was about five o'clock when the double-seated conveyance was seen coming down the little grade on Main street east just beyond Mill street [now Wallace Avenue South]," the *Stratford Herald* said. "'There they are!' some one shouted, and at once there was a mad rush for the carriage. It contained four people, but the crowd soon picked out the suspect in the person attired in a brown suit.... The scene then enacted was indeed a wild one, and under the circumstances it is little to be wondered that the man looked frightened."

The officers rushed the captive into the basement lockup unharmed, but the next night townsfolk collected into a more menacing force.

"There were shouts that McKay be brought out to explain where he was between 12 and 2 on Friday, or 'hang for it,'" the *Toronto Globe* said. "Constables Woods and Beatty drew their staves on the crowd and forced them back. It only wanted a leader to have set the law at defiance, for the constables were powerless against the mob."

One reason the crowd never turned violent, the *Herald* said, was that "the prisoner failed entirely to tally with [the police] description." On the other hand, under questioning, McKay gave a poor accounting of himself.

He said he spent Friday afternoon pruning marigolds on a farm but could not say where the farm was or name the farmer. When asked to show his earnings, he said he was paid with a meal. Police held him for two nights, then released him. Afterward, they discovered that McKay's real name was Nicholas Ackersviller, and that six weeks earlier he had escaped from the London Lunatic Asylum.

Finally, on Monday, three days after the killing, news reached Listowel of a more promising arrest. A tramp closely matching the police description had been intercepted seventy-five kilometres to the east at Cataract, in the Caledon Hills. Arrangements were being made to transport him the next day to Listowel station.

CHAPTER 9
"I Expected It"

JOHNSTON KIDD WAS TILLING a neighbour's field at the eastern outskirts of Listowel, near the racetrack, when he saw a stranger coming from the swampy wood. The date was Friday, October 19, the time shortly after two in the afternoon.

"Good day!" Kidd called, but the stranger turned his face and did not respond. He was wearing a tam-o'-shanter cap.

"It's a fine day!" Kidd called again.

"Where can I get a drink of water?" the man finally answered, still averting his face. Kidd directed him to Jane Ann Cattell's well next door. The woman, a dressmaker, watched the man through a window from four metres away, but she, too, could not see his face.

Shortly afterward, at two thirty, Henry and Sarah Leslie passed the stranger one kilometre east of Listowel, on their way into town in a buggy. He was wearing "a soft, black, felt hat," Henry Leslie said. Nobody mentioned seeing a black valise.

Between five and six o'clock in the evening, two cow-herding brothers, Thomas and Wesley Chamney, saw a tramp "walking about aimlessly," as Thomas put it, east of Listowel. He walked with his hands stuffed in his pockets and wore a tam-o'-shanter with a red tassel.

At a rise north of Listowel known as Smith's Hill, in his buggy, a farmer named Moses Smith passed the tramp, who called out for a ride. The farmer picked him up but almost immediately regretted doing so. Smith had just withdrawn a substantial sum of money from the bank, and the tramp, Smith said afterward, "looked as if he could cut up a person and as if he wanted to."

"Smith did not like the man's looks," the *Toronto Globe* reported, "and as [the stranger] climbed into the buggy remembered he had $75 in his vest pocket. [Smith] put his hand over his pocket with an involuntary motion, and the man looked quickly at him. Except for that one look he did not turn his face towards Smith at all during the mile or so they drove together. When Smith asked the man for a chew of tobacco, the man replied that he had none, and added, 'I have had a streak of d— bad luck.'"

Smith was travelling only as far as Gowanstown. During the trip, he recognized a carriage overtaking them as that of William Rodehamme, an agent of the Cone Coupler Carriage Company, who would be going all the way to Palmerston. "Being anxious to get rid of such an ugly customer," the *Atwood Bee* said, Smith persuaded Rodehamme to take the passenger, who climbed aboard. Around eight o'clock, Rodehamme let him off outside of Palmerston and a farmer fed him supper.

For the next three days, as police and groups of citizens detained and arrested tramps throughout southern Ontario, Chattelle somehow continued to wander freely. He had kept his face mostly obscured on Friday afternoon, but afterward proceeded much as before, walking in the open and chatting with people he met.

"He probably thought the mutilated body of his victim still lay concealed in the bush," the *Herald* later speculated, "and that he was far enough away from the scene of the crime to avoid suspicion."

Chattelle was moving fast. From Palmerston, he likely hopped a freight train, bypassing the hamlets of Teviotdale, Rothsay, and Bosworth, because the next person known to see him was Samuel Johnston in the village of Parker, twenty kilometres east of Palmerston and nearly thirty kilometres from the swampy wood. Johnston spoke to the drifter at seven o'clock on Saturday morning. News of the murder hadn't yet reached town.

"He was going toward Elora and asked how far it was to Toronto," the witness later said. "He had on the Tam o'Shanter cap. He said if he got to Toronto he could get a job out in a lumber camp."

By nine o'clock that morning, Chattelle had walked another eight kilometres to Alma, where an extroverted youth named James Laird was delivering meat for Andrich's butcher shop. Laird saw the stranger ahead of him and called out a greeting. Chattelle turned around. "He appeared startled when he saw the butcher lad swinging the hatchet," the *Herald* reported. "Seeing that Laird was not dangerous, he did not attempt to avoid him, and the two walked down the road together."

All Saturday morning, the day after the murder, people observed Chattelle as he wandered through Alma. General store owner B.C. Donaghy and millers Henry Cousins Sr., Henry Cousins Jr., and John Cousins watched the stranger walk down the street with delivery boy Laird. When Laird stopped to make a delivery at O'Neil's Hotel, Chattelle continued east toward the train station. He passed Alexander Jack's blacksmith shop. Jack and his assistant, William Pitt, saw him. At the station, agent James Cameron saw him, and section boss Moses Stinson spoke to him. Both Cameron and Stinson watched him drink from the station pump and proceed down the track. Nobody stopped or challenged him. Not until Monday would police in Alma detain their first suspect, the retired schoolteacher James McCabe.

At two o'clock on Saturday afternoon, John Little, a carpenter, saw the tramp sleeping beside the track three kilometres beyond Alma near Irvine Bridge.

Shortly after four o'clock somebody saw him on the tracks outside Fergus, and shortly before five David Mennie saw him on Fergus's St. David Street Bridge wearing a tam-o'-shanter with a red tassel. A Miss Forrester also saw him, and after five o'clock Chattelle called at a house on Tower Street, where Emma Samson gave him something to eat. That night Chattelle slept in a barn.

The next day was Sunday, two days after the killing, the day of the funeral. At seven in the morning, five kilometres north of Fergus, the tramp called at a house where Forbes Merre gave him breakfast.

At ten thirty, James Goodall, a grain dealer, saw a man in a tam-o'-shanter with a red tassel loitering at Belwood train station. So did Mrs. William Kyle. At about the time the funeral cortège was leaving the Keith farm for Listowel, Chattelle entered the station tool house, apparently to take a nap. Late that afternoon, heading east along the tracks, he called on a farmhouse in East Garafraxa, where a farmer named Cook fed him supper.

That night James Collins saw him in Hillsburgh. Collins called "hello," but the drifter "made no response or motion, and walked down to the creek as if to wash his hands," the *Toronto Mail* said. "He seemed to have a lot of clothing on, and kept his head down, stopping occasionally in his walk, as if to think."

The next day was Monday, three days after the killing. At fifteen minutes to noon, William Travis, a railway hand at Erin station, seventy kilometres east of Listowel, looked up from his work and saw a man approaching along the tracks.

"That's a pretty hard-looking seed," Travis said to his boss, Canadian Pacific Railway station agent J.D. Leitch. "I'll bet you a quarter that's the murderer of Jessie Keith."

Leitch approached the stranger. For a few minutes he engaged him in conversation, and although he let the man continue on his way, Leitch rode downtown to check the suspect's description in the newspaper. It matched perfectly. He alerted William Wilson, a police constable and bus driver, but Wilson hesitated. In 1894, rural constables were usually underpaid men with no expense budget. Wilson said he didn't know if he had the resources, or even the authority, to go after a suspected killer, especially one as wanton as Jessie Keith's. Leitch said if Wilson refused to go, somebody else would have to. Reluctantly, at one o'clock, Wilson set out with constable John Felker toward Cataract, six kilometres along the track.

Leitch also persuaded two men who were getting off a train, J.C. Blackwood and George Smith, to go after the tramp. In addition, Leitch harnessed his own horse and buggy to send Travis and another station hand, Tom Conboy, in pursuit.

Chattelle did not head straight for Cataract. He proceeded circuitously, sometimes following the rail line, sometimes leaving it and circling around before rejoining it again, doubling and tripling the distance he had to cover. It was a common ruse for a tramp under suspicion, the police chief in London, Henry Schram, later said.

"Tramps, as a rule, look alike and it is difficult to identify them," he told the *London Free Press*, "so when they are seen walking on the railway at a certain point, and two or three hours later come walking along the same way, it is puzzling unless one is onto the trick."

Travis and Conboy, however, knew who they were looking for. At the town line, Travis got out of the buggy and started alone down the tracks. Along the way, he called to farmers, asking if they had seen a stranger pass by. None had. Travis hurried along and eventually spotted a man ahead of him on foot. Travis started running to close the gap, as noiselessly as he could, and when he got to within a hundred metres saw the tramp drop what looked to be a small parcel. Travis chose to ignore it for the moment. He kept running, and when he got to within a few metres, the tramp spun around.

"Where the hell are you going?" Chattelle asked.

"To the Cataract," Travis replied and, placing a hand on the tramp's shoulder, told him to come along.

"He did some swearing," the station hand wrote afterward in a letter to the *Globe*. "He had a piece of turnip in one hand, and an open jack-knife in the other. He threw the turnip away, but still held the open knife in his hand, which he carried until we reached the Cataract station, a distance of about one and a half miles [more than two kilometres]. He appeared as if he wanted to use the knife on me, as he tried several times to step behind."

At the station, Travis telegraphed Leitch and waited for help. The prisoner gave his name as Amédée Chattelle, the spelling of which was to confuse authorities for years to come. Variations still circulating include "Almeda," "Almede," "Amede," "Chattel," and "Chattell." He gave his birth date as February 10, 1834, making him sixty years old, which was a lie, the same one he told at the barber shop in St. Marys. He was fifty.

Travis checked the prisoner's pockets. He found a woman's hairbrush and comb, a pair of women's black cashmere stockings, three pieces of soap, a small towel, a deck of cards, a pencil, and a pair of leather harvesting gloves. He also found a receipt from St. Marys for a pair of cottonade overalls. The knife Chattelle had been using to slice the turnip was an I*XL-brand jackknife with a wooden handle and a long blade, razor sharp. He had been carrying it, Travis later recalled, in his left hand.

When constables Wilson and Felker finally arrived, Wilson fumbled with the handcuffs. He managed to secure the first ring but had trouble with the second. "I arrest you in the Queen's name for the murder of Jessie Keith," Wilson said.

"I expected it," Chattelle replied.

Travis, in later testimony, expressed irritation over Wilson's seeming to take credit for the apprehension. "Wilson could not arrest anything," Travis said, and speaking of the moment Wilson put the handcuffs on the prisoner, he added, "He was trembling."

"Who was trembling?" Crown attorney John Idington asked. "Wilson or the prisoner?"

"Wilson," Travis said, and everybody laughed.

After the arrest, Wilson, Travis, and Chattelle returned down the railway tracks to pick up the discarded parcel. It turned out to be a tightly bundled article of women's clothing — a black cashmere waistcoat, or vest, trimmed with flowered satin brocade. Tucked inside was a red tassel.

The party returned to Erin. Wilson locked up Chattelle for the night and Travis — hero of the day — was sworn in as a police constable, assigned to escort the prisoner by train to Listowel.

CHAPTER 10
A Shower of Silver

THE NEXT DAY WAS TUESDAY, four days after the killing. Accompanied by the reeve of Erin, Charles Walker, Travis loaded Chattelle onto a baggage car.

At Listowel station, police were arranging for witnesses to view the suspect for possible identification. Their plan was to proceed secretly, but word leaked out, and when the train arrived at two twenty in the afternoon, three hundred people swarmed the platform. "The crowd had vengeance in their hearts," the *Stratford Herald* said. "Threats of lynching were freely uttered."

"It is improbable," said the *Toronto Globe* more skeptically, "that anything rash would have been attempted, because those present belonged to the substantial business men and cool-headed citizens."

As the crowd pressed around them, newly invested Constable Travis and Reeve Walker led the suspect in handcuffs from the boxcar.

Chattelle looked scared. "There were palpable evidences of fear on his dark-skinned countenance," the *Listowel Standard* said. Eventually, the throng eased back, giving everyone a better look. In almost every detail the prisoner matched the police description. He carried no black valise, but he was stout, stood about five feet, nine inches tall, and had a full chest, a short neck, stooped shoulders, and a weather-beaten complexion. Although he had been found at Erin to weigh 167.5 pounds, a guess of 190 to 200 pounds might be considered reasonable given the bulkiness of his clothes. He was fifty years old, not thirty-five as in the police description, but his hat — not a Christy but a tam-o'-shanter — made him look younger than his age. On his feet he wore new laced shoes with toecaps.

He fit the description, but on the platform events took an unexpected turn. For reasons never fully explained, as Chattelle stood cowering between his minders, a wave of doubt swept over the crowd. The hostility subsided, replaced by a groundswell of sympathy. Perhaps the townspeople were expecting the "human fiend" or "black-hearted monster" of the news headlines. Perhaps they had conjured up a terrifying image of somebody capable of slitting a girl's throat and mutilating her. Instead, standing before them, they saw only a vulnerable and visibly nervous homeless man.

"As he stood there, with the bright steel handcuffs on his wrists and a haunted look on his swarthy flat features," the *Globe* said, "the fickle-minded crowd, who a moment before were ready to believe him guilty, were at their first glance prepared to declare he was not the man ... although his appearance tallied exactly with the description of the murderer."

The *Globe* reporter also noticed something else. "There was in his bearing a self-possession and cunning beyond the intelligence of the ordinary tramp," the story said.

Not as impressed, the *Listowel Standard* described a "facial expression indicating craftiness of a very low order."

Seven witnesses were brought out, five men and two women. For their safety, the women were kept back and asked to observe from a flatcar. The seven included teenagers Armour Laird and John Attwood, the partridge hunters from Friday morning; delivery man Robert Morris, who had seen a tramp just before noon, ten minutes by foot from the crime scene; ploughman Johnston Kidd, who had greeted a man coming from the swampy wood on Friday afternoon; Jane Ann Cattell, who had watched the same man drink from her outdoor pump; and Henry Leslie and his wife, Sarah, who at half past two had passed a tramp wearing a tam-o'-shanter.

Of the seven, only Robert Morris positively identified Chattelle. The other six said the prisoner was not the man.

"No, no," said Sarah Leslie, the first to speak.

How does he differ from the man you saw? a police officer asked.

"Why, he has an innocent face," she said. "The man I saw had a face [so hard] that [it] would go through a stone wall."

Maybe her testimony influenced the others. Maybe the wave of doubt that had swept the entire crowd influenced them all except Morris. In any case, the prime suspect suddenly looked like a man falsely accused. Feelings of compassion further surged along the platform. Somebody suggested they take a collection. "One man threw a silver quarter at the prisoner's feet," the *Toronto Evening Star* reported. A second person threw a coin, then a third. Soon, everybody seemed to be lobbing silver quarters and dimes at the prisoner, who raised his hands, palms upward, to receive them. People noticed how big the hands were.

"He held up his manacled ham-like hands," the *Toronto Daily World* said.

"When he held [his hands] up for the silver from the crowd," the *Globe* said, "the attention of those around was attracted to their breadth and thickness, and suggestion of great strength."

Chattelle quickly gathered the silver into his hat. "God grant me justice in this country and I'll never come back to it again," he said, appearing ready to be on his way. The crowd would have let him go, too, the newspapers said, but Stratford police chief John McCarthy, who had taken charge, said discrepancies in the prisoner's story warranted further examination. McCarthy ordered Chattelle detained for vagrancy and guided him back to the freight car. It was bound for Stratford, which had a stone jail, one of the strongest in the province.

CHAPTER 11
The Legal Talent

PERTH COUNTY CROWN ATTORNEY John Idington stood as one of Stratford's most prominent citizens and looked the part. He was fifty-four years old, with a full beard and dark hair combed flat across the top of his head. He was also married with nine children, and was building what is recognized today as one of the most distinguished legal careers in Perth County history.

Idington graduated from the University of Toronto in 1864 and afterward co-founded a Stratford law practice with a local Liberal politician, Robert MacFarlane. As the town grew, so too did the firm. In 1875, after his partner's death, Idington built the first phase of the downtown office building that still bears his name, the Idington Block, part of what is known today as historic Festival Square. In 1885, as if to confirm his civic importance, he was chosen to deliver the keynote banquet speech marking Stratford's incorporation as a city. In 1905, eleven years after Jessie's death, he would also be named as a judge to the Supreme Court of Canada, on which he would continue to serve until the age of eighty-six, the oldest sitting justice in the British Empire. "He is 86 years of age and senile," Prime Minister Mackenzie King wrote in his diary. To ease him

Perth County Crown attorney John Idington, shown in this undated studio photograph, ranked as one of the most distinguished legal minds in Stratford's history. He was later named as a judge to the Supreme Court of Canada.

out, Parliament passed a law, which still stands, requiring Supreme Court of Canada judges to retire at seventy-five.

Idington would eventually lose his faculties, but at the time of the murder he possessed his full resources. Almost as soon as he heard the terrible news, he boarded a train to the swampy wood. He inspected the crime scene, issued the Wanted bulletin, coordinated the manhunt, and authorized Chattelle's detention for vagrancy.

He also oversaw the collection of physical evidence. On Saturday afternoon, the day after the killing, volunteers began combing the wood. At about two thirty, two men from Atwood identified as Dr. Rice and J.A. Roe, with a tracking hound, found most of Jessie's clothes tucked under the roots of an elm tree. Each item had been meticulously removed from the body after death.

"The underclothing was all taken off by being drawn over the victim's head or feet, and was turned inside out," the *Atwood Bee* said. "The dress was unhooked at the neck, and must have been done carefully, as the hook is very slenderly fastened to the dress. In no place on the clothing is a knife cut found."

Jessie's hat, shoes, and stockings were still missing. Near where the clothes had been found, searchers came to a small pool of water at an open drain. The water was tinted red with blood, as though the killer had bent down to wash after the butchery. Floating on the surface could be seen several bits of skin and chunks of flesh, some as big as half a thumb.

On Sunday, the day of Jessie's burial, searchers made another breakthrough. At half past nine in the morning, Listowel undertaker E.M. Alexander and a schoolteacher named Edward Chamney spotted an object on the north side of the wood. It was partly pushed under a log and covered with leaves and rotten wood, but one end was exposed.

"A great cry went up — 'The valise,' 'The valise,'" the *Stratford Beacon* said.

"A cheaply made article, of black American cloth," the *Listowel Standard* said. "It was burst along the top, as if by the pressure of too bulky contents."

The searchers tied the bag shut and sent it to Stratford for Idington. He opened it at his office, pulling out first a pair of bloodstained cottonade overalls, grey with brown stripes. They had been torn at the upper front thigh of the right leg and mended with a different-coloured material. Next came a black bonnet. "It was made of a satin fabric, much worn, and had a row of jet around the rim, corded silk strings, badly used up, four small black ostrich tips and a little crape in front fastened in with pins," the *Toronto Globe* said. "Across the top were three black bits of embroidery in the form of bands."

Next Idington pulled out a plain navy-blue skirt with braid at the bottom. In the pocket he found a linen handkerchief. One by one he recorded other items: a white petticoat, a blue blouse, a pair of men's white stockings, a pair of women's black stockings marked with the letter *N* in white thread, and a pair of muddied girl's shoes and stockings, later identified as Jessie's.

"It is very probable that the articles were stolen," Idington said of the bulk of the contents. He issued a bulletin listing them and urging the public to come forward with information on recent thefts.

On Monday morning, Charles Gowing and Archie Robinson poked the ground with sticks near the murder site and uncovered Jessie's black felt sailor's hat, stiff with blood, with the hatpin still in it. Inside the brim they found a pair of cotton garters, which had been cut, "the only articles of clothing that were removed with any degree of force," the *Atwood Bee* said.

Later the same day, in Cataract, William Travis added to the accumulation of physical evidence by retrieving from Chattelle the woman's hairbrush and comb, the black cashmere stockings, the other objects, and the I*XL-brand jackknife. Afterward, on the railway tracks, Travis and Wilson picked up the cashmere waistcoat and red tassel. Still missing was the Christy hat mentioned in the original Wanted notice. Asked about it later, Chattelle laughed and said it would never be found, and it never was. Also still missing were the excised body parts. They would turn up soon.

CHAPTER 12
The Celebrity Sleuth

AS SOON AS NEWS OF THE KILLING BROKE, the government sent for detective John Wilson Murray, one of the country's most famous police figures. He was a rare law-enforcement celebrity. "One of the most widely known men," the *Toronto Globe* said on his death twelve years later, in 1906, from a stroke at the age of sixty-five. "His fame was international, thousands of people knew him by sight, many hundreds prized the pleasure of his acquaintance."

Today, Murray serves as the model for fictional detective William Murdoch, protagonist in the long-running CBC television series *Murdoch Mysteries*. Murray, like the fictional Murdoch, was a pioneering Ontario sleuth who thought creatively and caught criminals by outsmarting them. The real-life detective, like the fictional one, also pursued his job with an uncommon tenacity.

"Hard work and consistent work," Murray once said, "is the thing which brings the largest share of what most people call 'good luck.'"

There are differences, however, between the two men. Toronto crime writer Maureen Jennings, who created the character originally for her series of novels, describes the invented Murdoch as "inspired by" rather

"One of the most widely known men," the *Toronto Globe* said of John Wilson Murray, Ontario's first provincial detective. Crime novelist Maureen Jennings used him as the inspiration for her fictional detective William Murdoch, made famous by the long-running CBC television series *Murdoch Mysteries*.

than "based on" the true-life Murray. Her Murdoch is a Toronto police detective. Real-life Murray worked for the Ontario government, the first person hired in a law-enforcement office that was to evolve into the Ontario Provincial Police.

The TV writers took further liberties with the character. When the first version of *Murdoch Mysteries* was being developed in 2004, *CSI: Crime Scene Investigation* reigned as one of television's most popular shows. In response, the *Murdoch* producers created what they privately called "CSI: Victorian," in which Detective Murdoch invents homemade forensic gadgets based on scientific advances of the day. He builds the "Day Light in a Box," fictional progenitor of the flashlight, and the "Numograph," fantasy prototype of the polygraph, or lie detector. Real-life Murray welcomed innovations such as blood analysis and the autopsy, but mostly he relied on the more prosaic techniques of measuring footprints, following cart tracks, and disseminating a description of the suspect.

The detectives also differ in appearance. Murdoch, played by Yannick Bisson, is matinee-idol handsome, a heartthrob who doesn't marry his love interest until Episode 100, in Season Eight. Murray, married with two daughters at the time of Jessie's death, comes across as a man's man, with a robust physique, a thick walrus moustache, and sad cocker-spaniel eyes.

"A fine specimen of manhood," the *Globe* called him, "a tall, sturdily-built man above the average height, and very strong…. [A] pair of blue, almost gray, eyes, [and] somewhat heavy eyelids inclined to droop, gave to him a mild and benevolent appearance, which was apt to deceive those who had no particular reason for making a close scrutiny of him. Those who took that trouble would soon find that … [those eyes] were keen, missing nothing of what went on around their owner."

The detectives differ, too, in personality. Where Murdoch is self-effacing, Murray was an unabashed self-promoter. He thrived on publicity. Reporters liked him because he passed on information, and people in general liked him not only because he caught criminals but also because he was congenial, sociable, and an entertaining talker. "A terror to the evildoer, a delightful companion to those worthy [of] his companionship," the *Globe* said.

Although originally from Scotland, Murray served in the U.S. Navy during the American Civil War. Afterward, he landed a job as a police investigator in Erie, Pennsylvania, and later for the newly completed Canada Southern Railway, which ran through southwestern Ontario between Buffalo and Detroit. He made a name for himself investigating robberies and criminal derailments, and in 1875 Ontario's attorney general hired him as the province's first government detective, assigned to solve high-profile crimes outside the provincial capital of Toronto.

Murray proved observant and decisive. On his first murder case, in the extreme southwest of the province near Wallaceburg, he arrived in time for the victim's funeral. A few nights earlier, Sarah Findlay had shaken awake her husband, Ralph, a mathematics professor turned farmer, telling him that the horses were stamping in the barn and that maybe thieves were trying to steal them. When Ralph opened the barn door to check, somebody shot him dead. Local police concluded that the victim had interrupted a robbery, but Murray was skeptical. At the funeral, while mourners waited for the clergyman to arrive, the detective started asking questions. A man named McLean said he had recently stopped by the Findlay place for a drink of water and found Sarah snuggling on the floor with William Smith, one of the hired hands. On the night of the shooting, although there were others in the house, Sarah alone had said she had heard the horses stamping. Murray confronted her and — before the funeral even started — extracted a confession. She and Smith had conspired to murder her husband and make it look like a botched horse robbery, she admitted. The interrogation, Murray said, went like this:

"'Out with it!' I said. 'Tell me the truth. I want nothing but the truth.'

"She looked up and her eyes were like those of an ox in whose throat the butcher's knife has been buried.

"'Oh!' she husked, in a hoarse whisper. 'Will you hang me?'"

The dialogue appears in Murray's autobiography, *Memoirs of a Great Detective*, a shamelessly boastful work published in 1904. The quotes are suspect, typical of the author's colourful writing, but the account is essentially true. Sarah Findlay and William Smith were not hanged, but both served time for murder. Smith died in Kingston Penitentiary after fifteen years.

On the day Jessie Keith died, Murray was investigating a series of barn fires in Chatham. He was fifty-four years old, the same age as Idington. Barns at four adjoining farms had burned to the ground and Murray suspected arson. When the attorney general's office sent a telegram ordering him to the bigger crime in Listowel, he hesitated. He had found identical boot prints at all four farms and was checking the boots of every man in the area. One of the farmers whose barn had burned down was wearing brand new ones. Murray never found the old boots, but with other evidence conclusively established that the farmer, Edward Kehoe, had set his own barn alight for the insurance money and had torched the others to deflect suspicion. Kehoe was convicted, but Murray always wondered where the old boots went. "If he buried them may their soles rest in peace," he says in his memoir.

The famous detective finally reached Listowel on Tuesday evening. He missed Chattelle's dramatic appearance on the train platform that afternoon and went straight to the swampy wood to inspect the crime scene. The next morning he boarded a train to Stratford. He met Crown Attorney Idington at his office and walked with him to the county jail to interrogate the prisoner.

In his book, with typical hyperbole, the detective offers his first impressions of Chattelle, colourfully portraying him as a monster equal to the horror of the crime. He titles the chapter "Almeda Chattelle, the Hairy Man." "When I looked at him he reminded me of a gorilla," Murray writes. "He was as hairy as Esau. As I studied him he seemed to look less like a gorilla and more like a donkey. He had huge ears and his face actually resembled the features of a jackass. He was very dark. He was not tall, but was broad and powerful, being under medium height, yet weighing one hundred and ninety pounds. He wore a woman's knitted jacket that had been stretched to bursting to cover his bulging muscles. On the back of his head was tilted a Glengarry cap. He walked with the peculiar swaying motion of a baboon when it rises on its hind legs and toddles across its cage. In fact, if the wild man of Borneo had been clipped close as to his hair, he would have been mistaken for this fellow's twin brother."

The passage mixes truth and fiction. The woman's jacket stretched over bulging muscles is made up. In fact, when he was caught, Chattelle had a woman's navy-blue waistcoat with white polka dots — the one stolen from William Maynard's clothesline in Stratford — folded inside the front of his shirt.

The Glengarry cap is accurate. The initial police description had Chattelle wearing a Christy hat — a stiff, black, brimmed hat of the type fictional Detective Murdoch sometimes wears in the TV series — but on his arrest the suspect was wearing a Glengarry cap, or tam-o'-shanter.

The "broad and powerful" physique is also true. He weighed 167.5 pounds, not 190, and nobody besides Murray compared him to a gorilla, but newspapers invariably portrayed the prisoner as a hulk-like figure. "When [Chattelle] was stripped for his bath, on his first being taken to the gaol, the officers were struck with the development of his muscles and the massiveness of his chest," the *Stratford Beacon* said. "His hands are abnormally large and his arms are knotted and hardened like those of a prize fighter in the pink of condition. His chest is ridged with muscular developments."

"His hands," the *Toronto World* said, "are of immense size, while his massive shoulders, now stooped, indicate that he must have been a veritable Hercules in his early youth."

"His flesh was firm and pink," the *Stratford Herald* said more graphically, "his muscles strong and flexible as a prize fighter's, answering every movement like so many responsive steel cables. There was not a weak spot about him. His sexual organs were abnormally developed. What with his gigantic hands, his Atlantean chest and his massive stooped shoulders, he is as powerful as Victor Hugo's Quasimodo."

One other detail in Murray's account rings true. "His voice was soft and low and sweet, a gentle voice," the detective writes. "A gentle, tender voice," he repeats later. Far from being the voice of a monster, it matched that of the haunted-looking man on the Listowel railway platform, standing nervously as sympathetic onlookers showered him with silver.

CHAPTER 13
The Interrogation

NOBODY SAW AMÉDÉE CHATTELLE kill Jessie Keith. To get a conviction, Idington and Murray would have to prove his guilt through circumstantial evidence. They would need to connect Chattelle to the crime scene and the recovered physical material. A confession would not necessarily help. It could be withdrawn before trial, and a trial carrying a possible death penalty might rule a confession inadmissible anyway. Besides, Murray always preferred to prove a case through detection. "I set out to prove the crime against him precisely as if he never had confessed," he says in his memoir.

To crack the case, Murray decided to canvass the region for witnesses. By train and buggy, he would track down people who had seen the man with the black valise before Listowel and the man in the tam-o'-shanter cap after Listowel. With their testimony he would establish a timeline. He would trace Chattelle's movements day-by-day, even hour-by-hour, on a trajectory that would place the suspect in the swampy wood at the time of the killing. Through detective work, he would also connect the tramp to the Ailsa Craig break-in and to the items recovered from the crime scene and from his person.

Idington and Murray began with an interrogation. It was Wednesday morning, five days after the murder. Chattelle awoke to his first full day of captivity at Stratford Jail. Murray arrived from Listowel by early-morning train. With several newspaper reporters, the government detective and the Crown attorney walked to the jail together from the nearby Idington Block to question the suspect for the first time.

Chattelle answered with a mix of truth and lies. At first he told the truth. One month earlier, he said, he visited his birthplace but left again to look for logging work in Michigan, passing through Ontario. On reaching Sarnia, he turned around and followed the Grand Trunk Railway line in a long north-easterly arc. At Lucan, he dug a well for a farmer named Joseph Hall.

The next part was a lie. After leaving Hall's farm, the prisoner claimed that he continued to St. Marys and Stratford, then turned straight east to Shakespeare and New Hamburg and hopped a freight train to Guelph.

If he went through Guelph, the interrogators asked, why were people in Palmerston sending telegrams saying they had seen him, which suggested he went through Listowel?

"To hell with Listowel," Chattelle said.

Asked about the black cashmere jacket recovered from the tracks near Cataract, the prisoner said he found it on the ground outside St. Marys. Asked why he threw it away, he said it was "not a proper thing for a gentleman to carry."

Where was he at noon on Friday, October 19, Idington and Murray asked.

"I can't tell what you're driving at," Chattelle said.

After the interview, Idington and Murray returned to the Crown attorney's office, where three key witnesses from Ailsa Craig were waiting. They had also arrived by early train.

Gordon McEwan, the boy about Jessie's age, told of meeting a tramp on the eve of the fall fair and giving him a walking stick. He also told of seeing the same man the next day wearing women's clothes.

The second witness, flax mill engineer Angus McLean, spoke of seeing a tramp lying on the grass drunk.

The third witness was Isabella McLeod. "An elderly and comely lady of kindly appearance," the *Toronto Globe* called her. "A woman of intelligence and discernment," said the *Stratford Beacon*. She told of the house break-in and listed the items stolen.

Idington and Murray showed her the recovered objects. No white apron, blue umbrella, or old pair of girl's shoes was among them. The black valise was hers, McLeod said. So was the black bonnet, decorated with small black ostrich-feather tips and a row of jet around the rim.

The men asked if she was sure.

"I have worn it long enough — I think I ought to know," she said evenly. "Those jet and feather trimmings were put on by me."

When Idington showed her two matching white petticoats, tension in the office mounted. One had been found in the valise, the other around Jessie's throat. Positive identification would connect the Ailsa Craig break-in to the slaying of Jessie Keith.

"Yes, it is mine," McLeod said of the stiff, bloodied one, picking it up. "I easily recognize it, for it was too short for me and I lengthened it by inserting a couple of inches of material below the bead band."

The one found in the valise was hers as well, she said. She further identified as hers the brush and comb taken from Chattelle's pockets when he was arrested. The cloth tam-o'-shanter cap belonged to her husband, Donald, she said. The black cashmere waistcoat that William Travis saw Chattelle drop on the tracks was hers. The red tassel recovered with the waistcoat came from the cap.

For Idington and Murray the morning had already proved productive. McEwan and McLean's testimony linked Chattelle to the house break-in. McLeod's valise, white petticoat, and other belongings found in the swampy wood linked him to both the break-in and the killing. The stolen McLeod items found on Chattelle's person in Cataract further implicated him in both. The failure of six out of seven witnesses to identify Chattelle on the Listowel train platform began to fade in significance.

"The jostling and the general awkwardness of the situation prevented them getting a cool, even look," the *Listowel Standard* said, dismissing the platform testimony, "and there was also the tendency when one or two had failed to identify, of others following suit from fear of being mistaken."

From the Crown attorney's office, Idington and Murray led the three Ailsa Craig witnesses to the upper west corridor of the jail where Chattelle was being held. Police chief John McCarthy joined them. McLeod had not seen her intruder, but McEwan and McLean positively identified the suspect as the tramp they had seen. Murray asked Chattelle about the valise and the clothing taken in the break-in. The *Stratford Beacon* reported the exchange this way:

> "Did you steal them?" he was asked.
> "The woman says I did," was the answer.
> "But, did you?" the question was repeated.
> "The woman says I did," he answered again, and that
> is all he could be got to say.

The *Toronto Globe* gave a more elaborate account. At first, Chattelle denied the break-in and claimed to have found the articles on a clothesline, the paper said. When Police Chief McCarthy pointed out that nobody hangs a hairbrush and comb on a clothesline, the prisoner admitted to entering the house and stealing the valise and other items. Asked about the missing objects, he said he tore up the white apron and tossed the blue umbrella on the railway tracks. Nobody seems to have asked about the old pair of girl's shoes.

The *Globe* also clarified a confusion about the waistcoats. Two were recovered: the black cashmere one dumped onto the tracks near Cataract, and a navy-blue cotton one with white polka dots found folded inside Chattelle's shirt, next to his skin. The first was stolen from Isabella McLeod's house, the second from the Stratford clothesline of Bank of Commerce manager William Maynard. The towel and the girl's stockings with the white "N," found in the valise, were also from Maynard's clothesline. A few items Chattelle was carrying were never claimed, including a pair of men's white stockings, a woman's linen collar, and a black straw bonnet with velvet trim.

Stratford police chief John McCarthy challenged the prisoner, saying nobody hangs a hairbrush and comb on a clothesline. Chattelle admitted to breaking and entering.

"It would appear that Chattel takes unaccountable interest in feminine belongings," the *Stratford Herald* said at one point, although in general the press paid little attention to Chattelle's taste for feminine attire.

All that day, Wednesday, other witnesses arrived at the jail. Listowel mayor Featherstone Smith came with T.F. Foley, the Stratford Massey-Harris agent. On the morning of the murder, they were crossing the railway tracks north of Britton in a carriage and saw a tramp carrying a black valise. Smith quietly made a joke, Foley laughed, and the man turned his face fully toward them, Smith said. At the jail, Smith identified Chattelle as the tramp, but Foley, apparently unsure, said only that Chattelle had the general style and manner of walking as the man he saw.

Robert Morris, the only witness to positively identify Chattelle at Listowel station, came for another look. "That is the man I saw, there is no doubt of it," he said.

E.O. Flanders, a resident of Wisconsin visiting friends in Newton, south of Listowel, arrived to give a statement. On the day before the killing, he spotted a man north of Newton and watched him carefully, he said.

"Mr. Flanders noticed particularly a peculiar expression which the prisoner's eyes assume at times," the *Beacon* said, "and was able to describe it very accurately, before he was allowed to see the man in the gaol."

Idington, McCarthy, and sheriff John Hossie walked Flanders through the jail's first two corridors. Flanders said he saw nobody he recognized. A *Globe* reporter was also with the party and in a single long paragraph described what happened when they arrived at the upper west corridor.

> There was seated Chattelle at one end of the table under the windows overlooking the splendid Collegiate Institute of the city. At the other end of the table was another prisoner, enough like him in some of his features and in his swarthy colour to be a younger brother or son. They were eating their supper from the bowls before them. "Stand up, Chattelle," said the Sheriff. The man charged with the most heinous crime ever committed in Canada stood up. His back and stooped shoulders were towards the windows. His hands, which are so abnormally large that they have been noticed by many people, were crossed before him. One of them has a cut in the back, and he keeps the wound covered with his other hand. The Sheriff told him to turn so that the waning light of the afternoon would fall upon his features. He did so, and eyed Mr. Flanders steadily. His manner was not defiant, neither was it merely dogged. His features, noticeably at the morning interview, though heavy, are very mobile, changing rapidly with his changing thoughts. "That is the man," said Mr. Flanders, pointing

to Chattelle. The prisoner, speaking quietly and deliberately, asked, "Will you tell me where you saw me." "I
saw you on the Thursday between Newton and Peffer's,"
said Mr. Flanders. Chattelle looked as though he did not
know where those places are, although he must have
become familiar with these names. "That is where you
camped all night," explained Mr. Idington. Chattelle said
nothing, and after a glance over the party turned and sat
down at his supper bowl again.

Other newspaper accounts mentioned the cut on the back of one large
hand, and Idington noticed something else. The fingernails were cut to the
quick. Chattelle said he always wore them short, but Idington said, no,
the skin around the nails was tender, as though the nails had been freshly
trimmed to remove traces of blood.

At some point during the day, the examiners asked Chattelle directly
about the valise. The prisoner admitted to carrying it with him, but said he
kept it with him all day Friday, the day of the murder, stashing it only that
night in the swampy wood, not at midday, as people suspected. Indirectly,
he placed himself at or near the murder scene on the day Jessie was killed.
Asked if he intended to return for the bag, he said he didn't know. Asked
if he had seen anything unusual in the woods that day, he said he didn't
know what they were getting at.

Late that afternoon, Idington and Murray spoke to reporters.

"There is no doubt we have the man," the Crown attorney said.

"We have the right man, you can depend upon that," the detective
said. Only "one link in the chain" was missing, Murray said — the body
parts. Finding them, depending on what they revealed, could lead to
further charges. That evening, the detective returned by train to Listowel,
and the next morning he and others searched a blood-tainted pond where
the killer was thought to have washed his hands. Bits of fatty tissue could
still be seen but no body parts were found.

From the crime scene, Murray left for Cataract. By horse and buggy,
he and Stratford constable Thomas Tobin set off to establish Chattelle's

movements from the swampy wood to the place of his arrest. At the same time, Listowel constable Robert Woods left to determine Chattelle's exact route from Stratford north to the swampy wood.

Details needed to be nailed down, but the newspapers essentially had their story. "It would be difficult to imagine a more forcible array of circumstantial evidence," the *Stratford Herald* said. "Proof has accumulated which no explanation compatible with innocence can dispose of, and which makes guilt as certain almost as if the murderer had been seen in the act," the *Stratford Beacon* said.

"The guilt of the Erin suspect is doubted by no one," said the *Toronto Globe*, "and the men who gave him silver would now give him a hempen rope."

Chattelle's mood darkened. He received a visit from two gentlemen, named in the press as Malcolm McFarlane, bridge superintendent for the Grand Trunk Railway, and His Honour Judge Woods. McFarlane was from Saint-Hyacinthe and spoke French. He happened to be visiting Stratford and, with the judge, came to test the prisoner's knowledge of the Quebec town he claimed as his birthplace. Chattelle's story checked out, and something in him provoked the same rush of sympathy in his visitors that overcame the mob on the Listowel train platform.

"Chattelle, if your story is true and you were not near the scene of the murder, there are people who will help to clear you," the judge said. "I, myself, would be one to contribute to a subscription fund to defend you."

"It's no use," the prisoner replied in his sweet, tender voice. "I'm in a deep hole and I'm going to stay there. You have too much evidence against me."

To examine that evidence, coroner James Rankin would resume his inquest in two days.

CHAPTER 14
The Coroner's Inquest

WILD STORIES BEGAN to circulate about Amédée Chattelle. Few hard facts about him had surfaced other than that he came from Saint-Hyacinthe and had wandered his whole life as a sailor and labourer. Almost nothing else was yet known and tall tales arose. In them, Chattelle appeared as a Forrest Gump–type figure, witness to some of the defining moments of his time. He helped the outlaw Jesse James and his brother Frank elude police by hiding them for two days in Texas. He struck it rich in the gold fields of California — British Columbia in one version — then lost everything. In 1889, he was among the few to survive the flood at Johnstown, Pennsylvania, when the South Fork Dam collapsed and killed 2,209 people.

"He said that he had witnessed many murders and lynchings in the West," the *Toronto World* reported, giving no source. The story could not have come directly from the prisoner, because Perth County sheriff John Hossie and jailer Hugh Nichol were refusing all access to him. Wary of a tendency among news reporters to romanticize outlaws, Hossie was keeping Chattelle under wraps.

The *World* decided to fact-check one story.

Perth County sheriff John Hossie, pictured in 1888, was among those who boarded the train to the swampy wood on the night of the murder. To deny any attempt to glamourize the accused killer, he severely restricted press access.

Nine years earlier, so it was said, the prisoner spent eight or ten months at an insane asylum in Taunton, Massachusetts.

"Investigation proves that Chattelle's story is a fabrication," the *World* said, blaming the suspect himself for the false report. "The *World* yesterday received a letter from J.B. Brown, M.B., superintendent of the Taunton

Lunatic Hospital, stating that Chattelle's name does not appear on the register during the past 25 years, nor do any of the attendants recognize the portrait and description forwarded to Taunton as that of any previous patient in the hospital. This disposes of the idea that Chattelle may have been in the institution under another name. The result of this enquiry will tend to show that Chattelle adopted the maniac plea [insanity defence] in order to save his neck, if possible."

With public opinion turning against Chattelle, authorities debated whether they should risk transporting him to the coroner's inquest. It was scheduled to resume at Listowel Town Hall on Friday, one week after Jessie's death, to establish whether investigators had enough evidence to charge him with murder. A jury would hear the case and deliver a verdict. A guilty verdict would send Chattelle to a magistrate's court to be formally charged. By law, the suspect's presence was not required, but if he did not appear no record of the inquest testimony could be used at trial.

In the end, authorities opted to take Chattelle to Listowel. Inexplicably, on Friday morning, they also chose to parade him five blocks through downtown Stratford to the Grand Trunk Railway station near the corner of Falstaff and Nile Streets. It was another fine autumn day. Sheriff Hossie took the lead. The prisoner followed, hands manacled, bookended by Stratford constable Thomas McCarthy, the police chief's brother, on his left, and constable John Coppin, from nearby Mitchell, on his right. Both were armed with revolvers. Behind them trailed the jailer, Hugh Nichol, and a police officer named O'Donnell.

"The crowd grew with every step," the *Herald* said.

McCarthy told Chattelle to stay close.

"I don't care," the prisoner said, according to the *Globe*. "They might as well kill me now as a month from now."

By the time the party reached the station, hundreds of workers from the railway shops had joined the throng, all of them vying for a look. A town drunk made a lunge for the suspect but missed, and McCarthy pushed Chattelle onto the train.

Already the car was nearly full. Crown attorney John Idington, who would be prosecuting the case, had taken a seat. So had coroner James

Amédée Chattelle, hands manacled, passes the Perth County Court House on his walk to the train for the coroner's inquest. Sheriff John Hossie, foreground, without his beard, walks slightly ahead. Flanking the prisoner are Stratford constable Thomas McCarthy, right, and Mitchell constable John Coppin, mostly hidden.

Rankin, along with a squad of newspaper reporters and a number of witnesses, including star witness Isabella McLeod, owner of the black valise.

At noon the train pulled away. Chugging north toward Listowel, it followed the same tracks the suspect was deemed to have taken a week earlier. It passed the tiny community of Britton, steamed across the front corner of the Keith farm, and approached the rise in the ploughed field where foreman Richard Stanton and his railway section men had spotted the scattered newspapers and pot barley.

"As the scene of the tragedy was passed it was pointed out to those in the car, including the prisoner, but he made no recognition of any kind," the *Toronto Mail* said. "Indeed, he looked out of the windows on the other side of the car in an unconcerned manner."

Just beyond the rise, at a spot at the edge of Listowel called Ballard's Crossing, the train stopped. A hackney carriage, or taxi, waited. Sheriff Hossie had arranged to have it spirit Chattelle directly to the Town Hall, avoiding the station, where hundreds of people from throughout the region were known to be waiting. While the train continued on an arc around the south end of town to the station on the west side, the taxi hurried directly to the hall on Mill Street (now Wallace Avenue South).

All business in Listowel was suspended. As the hackney turned the corner onto Mill Street, the prisoner's police escorts were surprised to see a thousand people gathered — a number equal to half the town's population. Angry cries went up.

"Hang him!"

"Lynch him!"

"Get the rope!"

Some spectators threw stones. When the carriage stopped, two or three men tried to grab Chattelle, but the police, clubs drawn, pushed him through the mob and got him safely into the basement lockup.

When the train station crowd realized the deception, they descended on the Town Hall as well, but the doors had already shut. Everybody not directly connected to the inquest was to be kept out. Some onlookers climbed to adjoining roofs to try to see through the windows, and shouts went up demanding to see the prisoner. Acquiescing, Sheriff Hossie escorted Chattelle upstairs to an overlooking pane of glass. "Lynch him!" people cried again when they saw him, but no stones were thrown and Hossie safely returned the prisoner to the basement.

In the main upstairs hall, fourteen of the original fifteen jurors took their places on a platform. William and Jane Keith and several close relatives took chairs near the front. The Keith children, Ida and Sandy, were not present. Officials in the hall included detective John Wilson Murray, police chief John McCarthy, and the post-mortem doctors, Samuel Rutherford and George Watson. Fifty-two subpoenaed witnesses sat ready to be called. Some had travelled up to eighty kilometres at their own

"One of the recognized leaders of the medical profession in this city," the *Stratford Daily Herald* once said of Dr. James Rankin, the coroner. On the night of the murder he immediately ordered an inquest.

expense to be there, but had done so willingly, the newspapers said. "There was no demand for compensation," the *Toronto World* said. "All seemed anxious to aid in the conviction of the perpetrator of so inhuman an act."

At precisely two o'clock, Coroner Rankin entered the hall and took his chair. Five minutes later, escorted by two constables, Chattelle appeared — still handcuffed, still dressed as he had been when arrested — and was seated at the front to the coroner's right. After a few preliminaries, Dr. Rankin changed his mind about keeping spectators out. He ordered that the hall be opened to as many people as could fit.

"The crowd … swarmed in over chairs and benches," the *Mail* said.

"The hall was filled to suffocation throughout the inquest," said the *Globe*. "In the audience, filling the aisles, and standing on benches, craning their necks and straining their ears and eyes with the men, were a large number of women."

In his capacity as Perth County Crown prosecutor, Idington rose to his feet. Over the next four hours, item by item, witness by witness, he meticulously laid out the evidence linking the suspect to the crime. Building on Murray's detective work, and the work of several police constables, the prosecutor stitched together every available fact and clue into a comprehensive timeline. Through eyewitness testimony, he precisely tracked Chattelle's movements, from the moment he came into view at Ailsa Craig to the moment constable William Wilson fumbled with the handcuffs at Cataract.

"Crown Attorney Idington produced the evidence," said the *Globe*, "handling the great crowd of witnesses with marked skill and dispatch."

"Detective Murray," said the *Mail*, "has won fresh laurels for his notably clever work in having presented such a remarkably consecutive chain of the prisoner's movements."

The prisoner mostly listened impassively. He watched like a spectator, not like somebody whose life was on the line. Sometimes, at Idington's request, he would get up and walk around, or put on a Christy hat or a tam-o'-shanter. At other times, in his sweet voice, he would interrupt a witness, but only to raise some trivial point, never to mount a defence.

"The prisoner's manner was that of a man with no personal interest in the proceedings," the *Globe* said. "He looked at the witnesses with the curiously interested expression of one wishing to see how near the truth the witnesses would tell. Sometimes he would say approvingly that a witness told the truth, and another time he would say, as if there was no consequence in the matter, that a witness was mistaken."

Idington asked two police constables to set the black valise on a table for all to see, along with other exhibits, including the clothes Jessie wore to town on the day she was killed.

"I recognize the valise as mine," Isabella McLeod stated, introducing the first pivotal piece of evidence. When the constables came to the navy-blue skirt found in the valise, McLeod held up one metre of matching cloth she had brought with her — left over from making the garment, she said. When the police displayed the bloodied white petticoat found around Jessie's throat, McLeod said she had made that, as well, repeating details she had given at the jail. Chattelle did not react.

"The prisoner showed not the slightest change of countenance when the [petticoat] was exhibited, but maintained his stolid demeanour," the *Mail* said. "[He] sat with his enormous hands alternately crossed in front of him or supporting his head with [his] elbow on the arm of his chair."

At times the testimony could be dull. Periods of tediousness set in as Idington called one witness after another, putting the facts on the record and fitting each piece to the timeline. At other times the evidence could be dramatic. One of the most excruciating segments came when Dr. Samuel Rutherford read aloud the searing post-mortem report, detailing the cause of death and the mutilation. So disturbing is the report that today the Stratford-Perth Archives restricts it to adults only.

"The feelings of the crowd were strung to a high pitch," said the *Globe*.

"During the reading of this graphic description of the fearful deed," said the *Mail*, "the utmost silence was preserved in the hall and all eyes were directed to the prisoner. His features became screwed up more than usual, and his eyes, which watched the witness furtively, blinked continuously from under the half-closed lids. The huge hands were clasped together, but not convulsively, and no tremor shook the prisoner's frame. The only motion was a constant swinging of his right leg, which was crossed over the left."

Dr. Rutherford said he had found no evidence of rape, a surprising statement given that the body parts had not yet been recovered and therefore not yet examined. At another point, the doctor testified that, based on the autopsy analysis, Jessie's killer must have been left-handed. He walked up to squeeze Chattelle's upper arms, right and left, and put the question to the suspect.

"That is correct," Chattelle said. "I am left-handed."

Dr. George Watson testified that the knife — the presumed murder weapon — had been washed, but microscopic and chemical analysis had confirmed bloodstains on the inside spring. Whether the blood was human or animal could not be determined, he said.

Three days earlier, on the Listowel train platform, six out of seven witnesses had failed to identify Chattelle. At the inquest, Idington questioned all but one of the seven again. Robert Morris confirmed his earlier certainty that Chattelle was the man he saw. Of the teenage partridge hunters, John Attwood was not present but Armour Laird was. Idington asked the prisoner to put on a stiff, black hat and walk around. Laird now said Chattelle was the man he saw.

Johnston Kidd went next.

"Would you have any objection to bidding the witness good day?" Idington asked Chattelle.

"Not in the least," the prisoner said, then remained silent.

"Say good day to him, will you?" Idington prompted.

"Good day," Chattelle said.

"That is as near the voice as I can remember," Kidd said.

Jane Ann Cattell did not see the man's face or hear his voice, but under questioning said the man drinking at her well resembled the prisoner "in build and style."

Henry Leslie said he still did not recognize the prisoner as the man he saw on the road. Sarah Leslie, however, revised her statement. At the train station, as the first witness to speak, she had firmly stated that Chattelle was not the man, because he had an "innocent face," not the hard face "that would go through a stone wall." At the inquest, she said Chattelle "looks very much like the man" she saw after the murder, but she could not identify him definitively.

At one point in the afternoon, as testimony from others continued, Dr. Rutherford and a police guard led the prisoner downstairs to examine the clothes he was wearing, the same ones he was arrested in. Why nobody had examined them earlier was not explained. The doctor found blood on them, specifically on the wristband of one shirtsleeve and the front of the vest and underwear.

What happened next spoke to the deeply ingrained sense of propriety that prevailed among the Scottish settlers of Listowel and Perth County. Not even the terrible tensions of the day could dislodge it. The moment was brief, and some reporters apparently missed it, or maybe they took such decorum so much for granted that they did not think to note it for their readers.

"Chattelle had been taken below to the lockup to be examined for blood stains on his clothes," the *Globe* said. "Three witnesses were heard without his being present. The prisoner was brought back.... The chairs which he and his guard had occupied had been taken during his absence. Several men on the platform rose to give him their chairs, among others, curiously enough, Mr. Keith, the father of the murdered girl."

Perhaps the most heartrending moment came when Jessie's mother, Jane Keith, stepped to the exhibits table. She wore mourning clothes — a long black dress and a black crepe hat.

"As Mrs. Keith picked up each of the articles to examine," the *Globe* said, "she threw them over her arm, all blood-soaked as they were, as though the fact that they had been her daughter's clothing took away any sense of horror."

One by one, she identified each piece — the red dress, the gloves, the garters, the black felt sailor's hat with two bands of velvet around the crown and a bow at the side. She spoke "in a firm voice," the *Globe* said. "Without nervousness," said the *Mail*.

"This is the chemise we put on her ten minutes before she left," the grieving mother told the inquest. "The stockings are my stockings, but she put them on that morning. The shoes are hers. The laces she cut for herself off a calfskin."

Idington handed the witness a purse found at the scene. "It is hers, for I told her she could not have much change left," Mrs. Keith replied, opening the purse and taking out a dime. She then held up the purse, and with a quaver in her voice, said, "I may take this?"

By seven o'clock, the inquest had been running for five hours. Dozens of witnesses had testified. Idington said he thought the jury had heard enough to reach an opinion. Coroner Rankin ordered the hall cleared of spectators, then, in the *Mail's* words, "summed up the evidence briefly, presenting in clear and forcible terms the most damaging testimony that ever was offered against a prisoner."

The jury huddled without retiring. Chattelle stood to stretch his legs and walked to a window. A large crowd remained outside, and when people glimpsed him a roar went up.

"Move away," Detective Murray told the prisoner. "Somebody might throw a stone."

"They may cut me up, or shoot or lynch me, I don't care," Chattelle said. "As well today as any time."

Within five minutes the jury members broke their huddle and a minute later the foreman announced a verdict. "On the 19th day of October, in the year of our Lord 1894, Jessie Keith was feloniously, willfully, maliciously, and with malice aforethought, killed and murdered by one Almeda Chattelle," he said.

The finding meant that the suspect could be charged with murder. Coroner Rankin accepted the jury's conclusion and dismissed the members, ending the inquest. Minutes later police magistrate James Terhune convened a magistrate's court. Witnesses were allowed to stay, but the general public was excluded. The magistrate read the verdict aloud and asked the prisoner to answer the coroner's verdict.

"Are you guilty or not guilty?" Terhune asked.

The *Globe* reported the moment this way:

> Every ear was strained to hear the prisoner's reply. It came in a tone so low that it was scarcely louder than a sigh — "Guilty!" His features settled into a look of stolidity. But not even a man of his stamp, though sunk into hopelessness by the afternoon's evidence, could utter

his own death warrant unfeelingly. He put his hand up to his eyes and rubbed them, as though to clear his sight. No one spoke or moved in the courtroom for several moments. All eyes were upon the man who, sitting there with his chin on his breast and his eyes staring into vacancy, had confessed himself the perpetrator of the most brutal murder in Canadian annals, and in the confession had put his foot upon the scaffold.

A dull formality followed. One by one, each witness briefly summarized his or her testimony for a record keeper, who took down each statement for the witness to sign or mark with an "X." The process dragged on. Idington invited to the front of the line those living farthest away, so they could catch the evening trains. Chattelle again sat with one leg over the other, swinging his foot and appearing indifferent. Finally, toward ten o'clock, the last witnesses finished giving their summations.

"Now that you have heard the evidence, have you anything to say?" Magistrate Terhune asked the prisoner.

"I have nothing," Chattelle said, but so weakly that Terhune didn't hear him.

"Do you wish to say anything?" the magistrate repeated.

"No," the prisoner said.

Terhune charged Chattelle with first-degree murder and ordered him kept at Stratford Jail until his trial in the spring.

It had been a long day. The court session was almost over, and, as officials readied the necessary papers, Mrs. Keith stepped forward from her chair beside her husband's to take one last long look at her daughter's accused killer.

"As she looked at the human monster, sitting so stolidly, her eyes, red with grief, seemed to look into the very depths of his inhuman heart," the *Globe* said.

Chattelle focused straight ahead, as though pretending not to notice her. Mrs. Keith returned to her seat, the magistrate signed the papers, and five police constables surrounded the prisoner to escort him from the hall.

The time was 10:15 p.m. A special train to Stratford had been ordered for 10:30, and it was up to police chief John McCarthy to get the prisoner there in one piece. He cuffed Chattelle and pulled the tam-o'-shanter down over his ears. The hall doors opened. An immense crowd pressed around the entrance, and the constables, batons in hand, pushed their way with the prisoner to a waiting carriage to the station. They arrived before the train and had to take the prisoner to the waiting room, where a throng of three hundred people caught up to them and surged through the doors. Many had seen Jessie's bloodied clothes and had heard the details of the mutilation in Dr. Rutherford's autopsy report, but they restrained themselves. Instead of attacking the prisoner they stood and stared. "It was, perhaps, something of the British reluctance to kick a man when he is down that showed itself," the *Globe* said.

Moments later the train whistle blew — at 10:30, exactly on time — and the commotion resumed. Once again the constables hustled Chattelle through the crowd, and on the platform cries of "lynch him," "hang him," and "here's the rope" started up again, although mostly from teenagers and from men who had been drinking.

In the melee, the police chief's brother, constable Thomas McCarthy, drew a loaded revolver and waved it above his head. A flying rock hit Chattelle, and he would have fallen, he said later, except the police were pressed so tightly around him.

"The prisoner received a blow from a stone thrown by some person, which almost brought him to his knees," the *Toronto World* said, "but he shrugged his shoulders and was apparently the least concerned man in the whole party."

Police Chief McCarthy actually did fall. In the pushing and shoving, he lost his balance and fell under the train when it was still moving, then scrambled to safety. The close call seemed to subdue the crowd. Having saved himself, the police chief helped Chattelle onto the train. A few men called for storming the car, but at the door Detective Murray joked with them good-naturedly, lowering the tension, and at 10:40 the train pulled out of Listowel station. One hour later it arrived at Stratford, and by midnight Chief McCarthy had his prisoner securely behind the stone walls of Stratford Jail.

CHAPTER 15
Confessions

AMÉDÉE CHATTELLE CONFESSED four times to killing Jessie Keith. At the inquest he pleaded guilty without elaborating. The other three times he gave details. At no time, however, did he admit to rape or address the mystery of why he mutilated the body. The reason would emerge only later, with the discovery of the missing body parts and a second autopsy.

The first confession, Detective Murray said, came at Stratford Jail two days before the inquest. Murray kept the admission to himself initially, he said, because he wanted to prove the case through detective work — through eyewitness testimony and physical evidence. After the inquest, however, he shared the information with reporters. "The prisoner stated that he did not know what possessed him," Murray said, "but he became animated by an uncontrollable, fiendish frenzy for the time being, and could not resist."

In his memoir, Murray embellishes, suggesting a redheaded girl aroused the tramp just before he attacked Jessie. Maybe he is referring to Carrie Lentz, the servant girl at James Gray's farm, who twenty minutes before the attack gave Chattelle a piece of bread, although whether she had red hair is not recorded.

"I had stopped at a house farther back on the road and a red-haired girl gave me a handout," Chattelle said according to Murray. "I looked at her red hair and then I went away, and when I met the pretty little girl it all came over me like a flash and I just grabbed her and carried her across the fields to the woods and cut her up. I do not think I was right just then, although I was all right before it, and I am all right now."

The second confession was the guilty plea.

The third came after the inquest aboard the train, although, again, the details cannot be fully trusted. The *Toronto Globe* and the *Toronto World* published identical transcripts, both presented as an exclusive interview with their own reporter. The *Stratford Herald* ran a slightly different account and referred to the interviewer as "the prisoner's interlocutor."

All three versions conform to the finding of three separate struggles between the killer and the victim. First, the killer struck Jessie on the head with a blunt object, causing her to drop what she was carrying and scatter the newspapers and pot barley on the tracks. Second, after being forced over the fence and across the ploughed field, the girl fought her attacker at the edge of the swampy wood, losing her white scarf. Third, deeper into the bush, the attacker slashed the girl's throat.

"Did you accomplish your purpose [rape the girl]?" the reporter asked the prisoner in the *Globe* and the *World* stories.

"No," Chattelle replied. "She resisted me on the track, and was too strong for me, and, after a struggle, I hit her on the head with a stone, rendering her insensible. I then half-carried, half-supported her across the field to the bush, where I cut her throat, and then inflicted the other wounds."

"What did you do with the [body parts] you removed?"

"I buried them in a field near where the valise was found. I can't describe the place exactly, but if a bloodhound was put on the scent it would find them."

"But why did you remove the parts?"

"I don't know. After I found I could not accomplish my purpose, I became maddened, and do not know what followed."

"Why did you strip the body?"

"I don't know."

"There was a strong case against you."

"Yes, and the witnesses told the truth for the most part."

"They say you have been guilty of similar acts before this?"

"No, never, and I would not do it again for all the world. I am sorry I killed the poor girl."

"Were you not afraid of being lynched?"

"I would not have cared. I might as well die to-day as to-morrow. What difference does a day make? I did it. I have confessed it, and I have got to die anyway, and the sooner it is over the better."

At this point in the interview, the *Globe* and the *World* said Chattelle became annoyed with people crowding around him in the train car and refused to answer further questions.

The *Herald* ran a longer, slightly different exchange.

"I saw the girl on the track," Chattelle said in that report. "She was a very pretty girl. I don't know what possessed me to do it, but I picked up a stone and carried it with me as I approached her. When I got up to her I struck her on the head. She screamed when I struck her, and that was the only outcry she made. She did not fall, but stood as if dazed, and bled freely from the wound in the head. Then I took her by the arm and led her to the fence. She walked freely with me and crossed the fence herself. She also walked across the ploughed field with me without much resistance. I just led her. When we reached the woods she nearly proved too [much] for me."

"Did you want to outrage her?" the interlocutor asked.

"I suppose something of that kind," Chattelle said. "When I found that I could not do anything with her, I got the knife."

"How did you get the knife when you could not manage her?"

"I don't know. I can't tell how I got it. I know I got it and cut her throat."

"Was she unconscious when you cut her throat?"

"No, she was still conscious when I killed her."

"Why did you mutilate her?"

"I don't know. I don't remember. I can't tell anything about that."

"And what did you do with the parts removed?"

"I hid them in the woods. But I can't tell where. I couldn't find them again. I don't know where they are."

The interlocutor pressed him.

"They are buried underground somewhere," Chattelle said. "A good bloodhound will find them sooner than I or anyone else."

The interlocutor asked why he committed the crime.

"I don't know," he said. "She was a pretty girl, a very pretty girl. It was too bad. I don't know why I did it and I'm very sorry for it."

The fourth confession came four months later. In February 1895, at Stratford Jail, Chattelle told his life story to somebody who wrote it down — the statement that William Keith managed to suppress and that *Listowel Banner* reporter Cy Bamford published in 1967. One page is missing: the one that apparently described the murder.

"According to Marshall Keith, the page was deliberately destroyed by the girl's father," Bamford wrote in his introduction. "He didn't want to be reminded of, or have the public know, the terrible things which happened to his daughter."

On the page following the missing one, Chattelle spoke of the aftermath.

"What possessed me to do the like of that I don't know," he said. "I never done it before in my life; you can telegraph anywhere I have been and you can't find anything of the kind, anymore than the time I locked up the [jailer]. I met this girl; after getting away from there I saw the section man — [it's not clear what he means here] — and a fellow plowing [presumably Johnston Kidd] and went straight down to him; I didn't hide myself; I went to him and got a drink of water [from Jane Ann Cattell's well]."

Farther down the page, Chattelle again reflected on the killing.

"I don't know what came over me that day; there was nothing more than common wrong with me that day," he said. "I take fits sometimes, but I don't know whether I had one that day. I get kind of puzzled in my brain when I have these fits, but I don't fall down. What I have done I don't deny it at all. I didn't mean to do it at all. If I could I would like the best in the world to redeem it, but it is too late now."

The confessions left no doubt as to who committed the crime but got no closer to explaining why Chattelle killed and mutilated her.

CHAPTER 16
On Trial for Murder

THE TRIAL OF AMÉDÉE CHATTELLE took place in a single day, on March 28, 1895, five months after the killing. If Chattelle were convicted, he would be sentenced to hang.

Well ahead of time, anticipating a crowd, police guards walked the accused from Stratford Jail to the Perth County Court House next door, at the head of Ontario Street. By eight o'clock, two thousand people were swarming the grounds. If they were hoping to get inside, most would be disappointed. By the time witnesses, potential jurors, news reporters, and family members were admitted, the courtroom was "packed to its utmost capacity," the *Exeter Times* said. Keith family members William, Jane, one of Jane's sisters, and sixteen-year-old Ida all wore mourning clothes. Young brother Sandy did not attend.

"He doesn't look like a human being at all," William Keith told the *Toronto Evening Star* on seeing the accused killer again. "He is the most brutal looking man I ever saw, and all the pictures that have been published do him more than justice."

Keith also spoke graciously of the support shown to his family.

"Our neighbors have done all in their power for us," he said, "and we have received letters, not only from all parts of the American continent, but also from all parts of the world. Some have contained considerable abuse regarding my so-called heretical doctrines, but I feel sure in their cases they misunderstood the unfortunate scene that took place over the grave of my little girl in which the Rev. Dr. Gunner figured."

The prisoner remained an object of contempt.

"Chattelle has not received the letters of sympathy that are usually showered on prisoners confined for murder," the *Evening Star* said. "The feeling against him is so strong that there are none to pity and the wish is freely expressed here that he may, whether sane or insane, pay the penalty of his crime."

Chattelle stood in the prisoner's dock under a magnificent two-tiered chandelier. After five months in jail, he had lost his darker sunburned complexion. He had not shaved for two weeks and had acquired a pair of spectacles. Otherwise, his features were easily recognizable — the same low forehead, hunched shoulders, thickset body, and oversized, powerful hands. He was also wearing the same clothes he had worn at the coroner's inquest — the clothes he was arrested in — and on the bench beside him lay the now trademark tam-o'-shanter, which Donald McLeod had never reclaimed. When he first landed in jail, Chattelle had said he was not a religious man, but beside him now laid a Bible with numerous bookmarks.

Promptly at nine o'clock, John Douglas Armour, chief justice of the Ontario Court of Queen's Bench, read the charge of murder in the first degree.

"Not guilty, sir," the accused killer responded in what the *Globe* called "a full, clear voice, and with remarkable distinctness."

Chattelle finally had a lawyer. The prisoner's half-brother, Prosper Chattelle, a shoe dealer in Saint-Hyacinthe, had retained H.M. East of Toronto, the first lawyer to act for the prisoner at any stage of the process. He had arrived in Stratford at three o'clock that morning with two medical witnesses, doctors A.R. Pyne of Toronto and W. Cockburn of Oshawa, both prepared to argue an insanity defence. As the trial was about to start, however, the lawyer and his client huddled for what the *Globe* called "a

A court sketch shows Amédée Chattelle standing in the prisoner's dock at the Perth County Court House. He elected to represent himself.

hurried conversation." East outlined his strategy, Chattelle rejected it, and East quit. Chattelle would defend himself.

"Counsel for the defence announced that he desired to withdraw from the case," the *Globe* said, "as the prisoner had mapped out a line of defence of his own, a defence with which [East] could not agree."

Crown prosecutor John Idington opened by reviewing the evidence, much as he had at the coroner's inquest. He started with the theft of the black valise in Ailsa Craig and worked his way step-by-step to the arrest at Cataract. The case might be circumstantial, Idington said, but so strong as to lead to only one conclusion.

Crown prosecutor John Idington opened by reviewing the evidence. It was so strong, he said, the jury could reach only one conclusion.

When hunter Charles Gowing told of guarding the body in the swampy wood, Chattelle began a cross-examination.

"Under what condition was it left?" the defendant asked, smiling, referring to the body.

"Covered with moss," Gowing said.

"Is that all you have to say about it?"

"That's all."

As at the inquest, Chattelle's interrogations led nowhere. Throughout the trial, he challenged witnesses on details but never on substance, and often drifted into nonsense. He was faking insanity, the newspapers said.

"Chattelle, with the cunning of the knave," said the *Stratford Beacon*, "began to play the fool for the purpose of exciting doubt as to his sanity."

When Isabella McLeod identified the valise and some of its contents, the defendant asked if she reported the theft.

"I told my husband," she said.

"Did you not notify the authorities?" Chattelle asked.

"No I did not," the witness said, perhaps mistakenly — the theft had made the papers. "I saw that the pane of glass was broken, and I knew someone had been there."

"That is not so — I did not break a pane of glass," Chattelle said, creating a stir by implicitly admitting that he had entered the home. The judge called for silence. "I raised the window gently," the defendant said, "and did not break anything."

Young Gordon McEwan testified that he saw Chattelle on the opening day of the fall fair wearing a woman's dress, hat, and veil.

"That's a lie. I had no veil on," Chattelle said. "Did you see a veil on me?"

"Yes, sir," replied the boy, who had also previously testified to the veil.

"I think you have said too much," Chattelle said, continuing with irrelevancies. "I had no veil on. It was broad daylight. I had more whiskers on than I have now, and no one said a word to me, though I passed through the crowd."

One after another, the slew of witnesses laid down the chain of evidence. Once again Dr. Rutherford graphically described the girl's wounds. Dr. Watson told of finding blood on the inside spring of the I*XL jackknife.

Chief justice John Douglas Armour presides at the murder trial. In pronouncing sentence, his hands trembled visibly.

Without a lunch break, the court sat into the afternoon, and at ten minutes to four Idington concluded his case. The judge invited Chattelle to respond.

"I have a secret, which I will give if the court wishes to hear it," he said, beginning a line of gibberish. "The subject is to go according to the Gospel. Any more information is to your own knowledge. I can give better developments later than at the present time. Such was the kingdom of heaven in the first place, and in the second place a corruptible church. That is as far as I will go."

Chattelle seemed to pause and the judge asked if he wished to say anything further.

"Nothing, except that I am pleased with the court as far as it has gone, but would rather not open the case unless insisted upon," he said.

"My complaints are that there will be objects either added or diminished. Further than that there will be nothing in it."

Invited specifically to address the jury in his defence, Chattelle said, "I throw myself into their tender mercy and care."

If the defendant was playing the fool, the judge wasn't buying it. In his half-hour charge to the jury, Chief Justice Armour "made no reference whatever to the possibility of the prisoner's insanity," the *Globe* said. At 4:30 the jurors retired. Ten minutes later they delivered their verdict.

"Guilty."

"That settles it," Chattelle said, showing no emotion as he stood in the dock, hands resting on the railing.

The judge asked the convicted killer whether for any reason he should not be sentenced. Beginning in 1967, Canada would abolish capital punishment in stages, but in 1895 the crimes of murder, rape, and treason could be punished by execution.

"Thanks, I have nothing to say," the killer said in a clear voice, without a tremor.

"You have been rightfully found guilty of a most atrocious murder," said the judge, whose own hands trembled visibly and showed more nervousness than the killer's. "I can only impose the sentence that the law requires in such a case, which is that the prisoner expiate his most infamous crime by a most ignominious death."

"I done it for a good purpose," Chattelle said nonsensically.

"Amédée Chattelle," the judge said, getting the name correct, "the sentence of the court upon you is that you be taken back from here to the place from which you came [Stratford Jail], and that on Friday, the thirty-first of May, you be taken thence to the place of execution, and there hanged by the neck until you are dead, and may the Lord have mercy on your soul."

"Correct, sir," the killer said, and sat down heavily.

CHAPTER 17
The Insanity Question

FOR ANY DEATH ROW INMATE, feelings of sympathy naturally arise. One hundred and twenty-five years later, doubts are inevitably stirred. Did Chattelle get a fair trial? Was justice properly served? Canadian history professor Karen Dubinsky of Queen's University gives voice to such questions. She goes so far as to say that Chattelle was wrongly convicted. "Race, class and sexual secrets" all but condemned him in advance, she writes in her 1993 book, *Improper Advances: Rape and Heterosexual Conflict in Ontario, 1880–1920*. Being a lower-class, cross-dressing, transient French Canadian, she argues, Chattelle didn't stand a chance. He was victimized by the system, or what she contemptuously calls "Anglo-Saxon law," "the Anglo-Saxon legal system," and "the British system of justice."

Dubinsky might be extreme in her contempt for British legal institutions, but her thesis plays to a widespread stereotype of Canadian Victorians as prudish and bigoted. In the Chattelle case, the stereotype is unfair. The killer's fetish for female clothing drew almost no notice — not from the detective, not from the prosecutor, and not from the press. Similarly, the killer's social status as a tramp was referred to as a fact, not a judgment, and his French-Canadian heritage played no apparent role at all. Speaking with a French accent must have been rare in Perth County in 1894, but the only witnesses reported to have mentioned an accent were partridge hunter Armour Laird and James Gray's servant girl, Carrie Lentz. They did so not out of prejudice, but to help identify the killer. Nothing disapproving was reported of French Canadians whatsoever. On the contrary, the *Toronto Globe* took the trouble to send a reporter to Saint-Hyacinthe, and published a positive evaluation of Chattelle from his former boss, a foreman named Lefebvre. "He attended to his business," Lefebvre said. "[He] never had any quarrel of any kind with the other men ... and I never heard him tell any stories about women."

Dubinsky further suggests that Jessie, being an "innocent girl," was viewed inappropriately as a "saintly martyr" — Dubinsky's words. In fact, the girl's age and innocence stood as important considerations. Her age made the crime an act of pedophilia, among other atrocities, and her innocence defined the attack as entirely unprovoked.

Accusations of bias might apply to the press. News reports universally judged Chattelle guilty until proven so in a court of law, but they did so in keeping with the standards of the time, not as an exception.

Chief Justice Armour of the Ontario Court of Queen's Bench rightly established who killed Jessie Keith. Amédée Chattelle killed her, and did so in close to the most demonic way imaginable. The verdict had nothing to do with race, class, or a fancy for women's undergarments. It sprang from the facts of the case. The system worked. The police tracked down their man, Murray rounded up witnesses and established a timeline, and Idington laid out an irrefutable body of circumstantial evidence. The crime might have riled the populace into a frenzy, but townsfolk and farmers ultimately restrained themselves from harming the prisoner, to the point where the father of the murdered girl stood to offer the accused killer a chair.

On conviction the sentence was never in doubt. Such an extreme crime merited the maximum penalty. In all of southwestern Ontario, thirteen people had been convicted of murder in the previous eighteen months, but not one had been executed. In Perth County, Chattelle would be the first.

One question lingers, however: Was Chattelle insane? No lawyer had acted on his behalf. No psychiatrist had certified his fitness to stand trial. No judge had directly addressed questions about the prisoner's mental state.

Professor Dubinsky writes that "it appears likely" that Chattelle was insane, but as evidence she cites false information that he "had spent several years in an asylum."

University of Toronto law professor Martin Friedland, in his 1986 book, *The Case of Valentine Shortis*, about an 1895 Quebec murder, mentions Chattelle several times and gives his opinion that the killer "appeared to be really crazy." The registrar of the Toronto medical college wrote after the trial, Friedland says, that Chattelle suffered from a form of insanity called cerebral paresthesia sexualis, and nine other Ontario doctors swore affidavits to the same effect. None, however, had examined Chattelle. None had even met him. Judge Armour rejected the affidavits as unpersuasive, as did a panel of ten federal cabinet ministers, and the government refused to reopen the case.

In his confessions, Chattelle raised the possibility of temporary insanity. Detective Murray said the killer spoke to him of being "animated by an uncontrollable, fiendish frenzy for the time being."

Four months later, in his written statement, Chattelle put it slightly differently: "I take fits sometimes, but I don't know whether I had one that day. I get kind of puzzled in my brain when I have these fits, but I don't fall down."

After the trial, the *Stratford Beacon* published a further account of the killer's possibly deranged state of mind, in a sense a fifth confession. While once serving time as a vagrant, the paper said, Chattelle understood that his mission in life was to rescue people like himself from their misery. "The rest of his life was to be devoted to the relieving of the oppressed," the paper said. On the railway tracks a further revelation apparently came to him: "He picked up two stones and carefully weighed them. The lighter one he cast away; the heavier one he retained. Then he met Jessie Keith and an irresistible impulse came upon him to strike her and he did so. He had no unworthy motive in doing so; it was part of his work. Being asked why he had begun his mission for the relief of the oppressed by the murder of an innocent little girl he replied that he had no control over his own soul."

The story echoes Chattelle's words to the judge: "I done it for a good purpose."

The *Beacon* did not disclose the source of its account, but in 1945 Toronto historian Edwin Clarence Guillett named the informant as Father Downey, a Roman Catholic priest who had been visiting the accused killer in jail. Downey at first believed the insanity theory, Guillett wrote in his booklet, *The Mutilation of Jessie Keith*. Later, however, the priest changed his mind, concluding that "the doomed man was cunningly pretending insanity until all hope was gone." Without quoting Downey, the *Beacon* made the same point: "Now that [Chattelle] sees no hope of reprieve, he has thrown off the mask and is as sane a man as can be found anywhere."

Today, a trial judge would make a greater effort to establish the killer's mental state. If Chattelle were found fit to stand trial and insisted on representing himself, the judge would appoint a "friend of the court," a lawyer to protect Chattelle's legal rights and inform the court on aspects of the case. A modern trial, however, might also introduce evidence damaging to Chattelle's case that went unexamined in 1895.

"They say you have been guilty of similar acts before this," the interviewer for the *Globe* and the *World* stories asked on the train after the inquest.

"No, never," the prisoner replied, but a fifty-year-old man for the first time compulsively attacking a girl seems unlikely.

"Chattelle claims that he never previously committed this [type of] crime," the *World* said. "The probabilities are, however, that he has done so."

Police Chief McCarthy said he also suspected a prior serious offence. "Chattelle had a way of drawing his custodians into him and crouching between them as shields from violence, which could only have been of experience," he told reporters.

A modern trial might also raise the question of premeditation. In St. Marys, Chattelle bought a razor-sharp knife, and the next day a man matching his description attacked a young woman on the St. Marys–Stratford road, where Chattelle would have been at the time (see chapter 2).

William Keith observes the trial proceedings. "I think there's a screw loose some-where," he said of his daughter's killer, "but I believe he knew what he was doing."

Neither the purchase of the murder weapon nor the attack the next day was introduced into evidence.

In 1895, the main question considered was whether Chattelle knew right from wrong. Three days after the trial, jail surgeon Dr. J.M. Dunsmore publicly expressed his opinion, shared by many. "As the law defines insanity, he is perfectly sane," the surgeon told the *Globe*. "An insane man takes no heed of consequences. He does not know what he is doing, and does not care for results. The murderer of Jessie Keith was conscious that he was committing an illegal act. An insane person would not have acted as Chattelle did. He hid the body of the murdered girl, hid the clothing, hid the black valise, and stole away to escape detection."

Detective Murray never bought Chattelle's allusion to temporary insanity. "I was satisfied that he was aware of what he was doing, at the time he did it and thereafter," he says in his memoir.

A reporter asked William Keith what he thought of the insanity theory. "I think very little of it, but he worked his game pretty well," he said of the killer. "I think there's a screw loose somewhere, but I believe he knew what he was doing when he butchered my little girl and is responsible for his crime."

Several weeks after the trial, Chattelle's family rehired Toronto lawyer H.M. East. He filed a formal appeal to the Ontario justice ministry arguing that Chattelle, as the *Globe* put it, "is afflicted with a peculiar form of insanity mentioned in the works of a German expert," and therefore not criminally responsible. The ministry rejected the petition and preparations went ahead for the execution.

CHAPTER 18
Ropes and Pulleys

THE DATE WAS SET for Friday morning, May 30, 1895. On Thursday afternoon the train from Toronto delivered the hangman, John Radclive. "A stout, well-built Englishman, with ruddy cheeks, heavy dark moustache and a pronounced accent," the *Stratford Beacon* called him. "He is neatly dressed, jaunty in his manner, voluble in his conversation and always ready with his joke or story or his repartee."

Beginning in 1892, Radclive served as Canada's first professional executioner. He would die of alcoholism in 1911 at the age of fifty-five, emotionally tortured by visions and nightmares and by then a vocal opponent of capital punishment. At the time of Chattelle's execution, however, he still thought of himself as a public benefactor, dedicating his skill and craft toward quick, merciful executions of convicted criminals deemed a danger to society.

"Do you think any of them suffer much?" a Stratford citizen asked him on the eve of Chattelle's hanging.

"Well, I never heard any of them complain," he said.

After checking into the Albion Hotel, Radclive walked up Ontario Street to the jail yard to supervise preparations. His method at the time was not to drop his client from a scaffold through a trap door. His simple rigs had no scaffold and no trap door. Instead, he instructed workmen to plant two uprights into the ground joined by a single crossbeam, like football goalposts, with one end of the crossbeam extending beyond the uprights. The condemned person would stand on the ground between the uprights with a rope around the neck. The rope would run through pulleys to a lead counterweight hanging from the extended part of the crossbeam. When Radclive released the counterweight, it would yank the rope, and the noose would fling the condemned person into the air. The action would snap the neck either with the initial jerk or with the final yank of the rope on the way down. The idea was to break the neck without detaching the head from the body, an outcome that required prior calculations concerning the subject's weight, build, and neck characteristics. For the Stratford execution, Radclive ordered a hefty counterweight of 160 kilograms.

Chattelle likely saw the hanging rig being built. Guards had transferred him from the upper west corridor to the westernmost cell on the ground floor, facing the construction twenty metres away. If he couldn't see the carpenters, he would at least have heard them hauling materials into the yard and hammering them into place.

Understandably, he was getting nervous. Two weeks earlier, he had had a disturbing dream, the *Beacon* reported, not naming a source (likely Father Downey). The dream was described this way:

> He [Chattelle] thought that he sat alone in a small but beautiful boat. The boat was on a river, he knew not where, and although he has travelled nearly all over the world Chattelle says he never really saw such fine scenery as he fancied surrounded the banks of the river. Just beside the water the ground appeared to be somewhat flat, but as it receded from the banks it began to rise gradually till at a great distance majestic, snow-capped mountain peaks could be seen rising almost, the dreamer thought, to Heaven. Chattelle imagined that the river

was clear as crystal, was several feet deep and had a bottom of the finest gravel. Its current was swift and was sufficient to bear along the boat without its occupant putting forth any effort. Chattelle sat in the stern of the boat with his head upright as it glided swiftly on its way. At length he saw in the distance a bridge which was very high above the water. As he approached it he lowered his head in order that he might pass safely underneath. Alas for human hopes! He did not strike the framework but a wire caught him in the neck and in an instant he was suspended between Heaven and earth, or rather between sky and water. He suffered untold agonies for a few seconds and then awoke.

On the evening before the hanging, Chattelle ate what was described as "a hearty supper" of porridge and bread and butter. Part of the night he spent composing a speech he planned to recite before having the black hood placed over his head. He would say something about his life, acknowledge the justice of his punishment, and ask forgiveness from God and society, especially William Keith, for the irreparable wrong he had committed against him and the Keith family.

The next day was hanging day. Chattelle ate a breakfast of two poached eggs, toast, coffee, and a glass of brandy. He was offered ham but turned it down because the execution fell on a Friday, and he now considered himself Roman Catholic. By tradition, Catholics abstained from meat on Fridays as a penance to mark the day of Christ's death.

At a quarter to seven Father Downey arrived. Outside a crowd began to gather. Canada had banned public executions in 1870, but about three hundred people stood outside the jail on the sidewalk or sat on the lawn. A few boys and men stood on the roof of the high school next door, but none could get a view over the prison wall. At seven thirty, executioner Radclive again walked up Ontario Street from the Albion Hotel, this time smoking a cigar. Displaying his jaunty facade, he even paused to greet people he had met socially the evening before.

At a quarter to eight, the bell of nearby St. Joseph Catholic Church began to toll. In the jail yard about fifty people waited, including town officials, newsmen, and various special visitors. Nobody from Chattelle's family attended but William Keith was there — not out of feelings of revenge, he said, but a wish to see for himself the law carried out. "I think," he said, "that it is better for the world that a man who would commit such a crime as he did should be put out of it."

Radclive checked the ropes and pulleys one last time, then entered a door to the cells from the prison yard. At the stroke of eight the door reopened. Out stepped sheriff John Hossie, who seven months earlier, on the night of the murder, had been among those to board the train for the swampy wood. Next came the chief jailer, Hugh Nichol, an assistant named Mr. Allan, jail surgeon Dr. Dunsmore, and Father Downey, who was reciting prayers. Then Chattelle stepped into the spring sunlight. He had grown a beard. He wore the same clothes he had worn during his arrest and trial, but without a jacket or the tam-o'-shanter hat. His head was bare, his large, meaty hands were cuffed, and two police guards held him by either arm. The executioner brought up the rear. The *Globe* reported the moment this way:

> Chattelle's face was pale and bloodless, with a pallor seldom seen save on the face of the dead. The ashen hue was heightened by the grizzly, iron-grey beard, which had grown since his incarceration, and which had so changed his appearance that a casual observer would not have recognized him. The cheeks, too, were sunken, and the eyes wore a hunted, haggard look, which told more eloquently than words how terrible had been the mental anguish of the past few weeks. Though the guards held him on either side, he walked firmly and evidently without need of the support, and, apparently oblivious to the presence of the onlookers, he was repeating the responses to the priest's prayer in low, audible tones.

Once Chattelle reached the hanging rig, everything happened quickly. He was ready to deliver his speech but Radclive stopped him. "If they have anything to say," the executioner explained afterward, "let them say it to the sheriff or the clergyman before they come out."

Father Downey began reciting the Lord's Prayer. "Our Father, who art in heaven," he said as Radclive wrapped a leather strap around the condemned man's legs. "And forgive us our trespasses," the priest said as the hangman placed a black hood over the condemned man's head and adjusted the noose. At four minutes past eight, as Downey began the line, "but deliver us from evil," Radclive released the counterweight, flinging the condemned killer three metres into the air. A moment later, Amédée Chattelle hung lifeless from the end of the rope, his feet a few centimetres from the ground.

"An involuntary shudder ran through the little group of silent spectators as the relaxing muscles gave two or three convulsive twitches to the body," the *Globe* said, "but there was not a sound or sign of life as Dr. Dunsmore seized the limp right wrist and felt for a pulse."

As a signal to the public, the bells of St. Joseph's rang again and a black flag flew at half-mast for one hour outside the jail. That same morning, Chattelle was buried in the prison yard, the grave left unmarked. Nobody had applied to receive the body.

One hundred and fifteen years later, in 2010, workers upgrading the prison foundations in the yard discovered the bones of two executed prisoners. One was Frank Roughmond, hanged in 1909 for the rape and murder of a sixty-six-year-old farmwife, Mary Peake, outside Stratford. The other was Chattelle. The remains of both were reinterred in unmarked graves in section 25-C of Stratford's Avondale Cemetery.

CHAPTER 19
Two Autopsies

NINE DAYS AFTER THE MURDER, on a Sunday, H.L. Howell of London, Ontario, led a search party for the missing body parts. He brought a dog. The volunteers were on the point of abandoning the hunt, the *Atwood Bee* said, when Howell noticed the dog "making a slight demonstration" at the foot of an elm sapling near a fence. Carefully brushing away the leaves, he discovered the missing organs.

Listowel physicians Samuel Rutherford and George Watson performed two separate autopsies. They completed the first at the Keith farmhouse hours after the body was discovered, and stated their findings at the inquest and the trial in every sickening detail. The specifics of their second post-mortem examination were withheld from the public but can now be told.

In their initial hand-written report of tightly spaced characters, the doctors outlined evidence of a series of ruthless attacks. They enumerated two bruises on the left side of the forehead, a large, swollen bruise above the right eye, superficial cuts to the face, and a deep stab wound below the lower lip, as though the girl had ducked to avoid a stab to the throat. They also noted a large swelling at the crown of the head, as though from a blunt instrument, such as a rock. Blood had flowed freely from both the head and nose, the physicians said, matting the hair and bloodying the mouth and chin.

Death, they said, resulted from the loss of blood caused by four slashes to the throat with a sharp instrument. They were terrible wounds. The lacerations completely severed the external jugular veins on both sides of the neck and the internal jugular on the right side. They also cut the wind-pipe just above the vocal chords. "All the cavities of the heart were com-pletely empty," the report said. The girl likely died within thirty seconds.

After death, the abdomen had been subjected to a series of sweeping vertical and horizontal slashes, from the navel downward. Some of the organs had been gouged out and discarded, including the uterus, the external genitals, and part of the bladder. The Jack the Ripper theory, later discredited, sprang from the sexual mutilation. The Whitechapel murders had also included deep throat slashes, abdominal and genital-area mutilation, and removal of internal organs, including the uterus.

Speaking to reporters before dawn at the Keith farmhouse, Dr. Watson speculated that the girl had also been raped. Whether the violation had come before or after death he could not determine, he said, without exam-ining the missing body parts.

"My opinion is that the fellow covered the body so carefully with a view of keeping it hid until spring," the doctor also said, "when it would be decomposed beyond recognition, and the removal of the organs would prevent the discovery of the sex."

After the missing parts were discovered, Drs. Rutherford and Watson examined them microscopically. Again in medical detail, shockingly graphic to the layman, they confidentially recorded their findings: "In the vagina was found a yellowish semi-transparent sticky substance of a somewhat fluid consistence which resembled semen." Microscopic analysis failed to confirm sperm cells, the doctors said, but the fluid was distinct from surrounding decomposed membrane.

At the inquest, Dr. Rutherford stated that Jessie had likely fended off her attacker's intended rape. From the second post-mortem he drew a more repulsive conclusion, which he expressed obliquely to the press.

"He gives it as his opinion that the girl was undoubtedly outraged," the *Atwood Bee* said, "but whether before or after death it was impossible at that moment to determine."

Putting together the forensic analysis with the killer's confessions, the events come into sharper focus. Jessie was thirteen years old, almost fourteen, and physically mature for her age. Chattelle was fifty, muscular, with powerful hands. They approached each other on the railway tracks. Maybe he tried to engage her in conversation, or maybe he was gruff. In any case, she shrank from him, and he picked up a rock and struck her on the head.

Jessie staggered. Dazed and bleeding, she dropped the newspapers and pot barley. Chattelle, still clutching the black valise, hauled her with his other arm and half led, half dragged her over the fence and across the field into the swampy wood. Frantically, Jessie fought back. In the struggle, Chattelle ripped off her scarf, the pin still fastened. Somehow, he forced her more deeply into the bush. He tried to knock her to the ground but she kept fighting. Fed up, he swung at her with the knife, going for the throat. She ducked. The knife stabbed her chin. He took several more swipes, slashing her throat, and within thirty seconds the girl was dead. The killer tied one of Mrs. McLeod's petticoats around her neck to cover the gore and meticulously undressed the body. He then sexually desecrated the corpse and excised the genital area.

Altogether, Chattelle spent nearly two hours in the swampy wood. He changed out of the brown-striped grey overalls, now bloodstained, and stuffed them into the valise. They would be the first item Idington would pull from the bag. Chattelle put on his extra trousers and exchanged the Christy hat, which was never found, for the tam-o'-shanter. He gathered moss and leaves to cover the body, stashed the valise under a log, and washed his hands in the pool at the open drain. About the time that William Keith and the section men were crossing the ploughed field toward the wood, the killer emerged into the eastern outskirts of Listowel, where ploughman Johnston Kidd wished him good day.

Crown Attorney Idington and Detective Murray must have felt confident they had evidence strong enough to convict Chattelle and see him hang. They never released the second report and never charged Chattelle with defiling the corpse. As far as the public was concerned, Dr. Rutherford's statement at the inquest that Jessie had successfully fended off the rape was left at that.

"While defending her honor she lost her life," her tombstone reads.

CHAPTER 20
The Healing

AFTER THE MURDER, the people of Perth County and throughout southwestern Ontario donated money for a monument to mark Jessie's grave. In commemorating the girl's short life, they sought to comfort the Keith family and salve their own sorrows. With the contributions, organizers bought a block of marble from one of the world's top quarries, near Carrara, in northern Italy, the one that produced the stone for Michelangelo's *David*. The marble was pure white, without veins, of a variety since mined to exhaustion at Carrara. Organizers also commissioned an Italian sculptor, whose name has been lost, to carve a statue of Flora, the Roman goddess of flowers, springtime, and youth, scaled to the size of a thirteen-year-old girl. In Listowel, local stonemason Robert Kemp mounted the statue on a column of polished granite from Aberdeen, Scotland, the Keiths' ancestral home. He also mounted the column on a double freestone base from Ohio. "A beautiful and costly work of art," the newspapers said, without specifying how costly.

The monument still stands. It is one of the tallest in Fairview Cemetery and by far the most majestic. Although weathered, the Goddess of Flora statue remains a work of exquisite tenderness, a figure of enduring grace and beauty to mark one of the ugliest episodes in Perth County history.

JESSIE KEITH MEMORIAL.

ERECTED MAY 24 1896.

"We miss her at home," says the inscription on the granite column from Aberdeen, Scotland, supporting the statue of the Roman Goddess of Flora. The photo appeared in the program notes printed for the official unveiling.

In total, the structure rises to 3.5 metres. The statue itself stands 1.4 metres, although Jessie stood slightly taller. With her left hand, the goddess cradles a wreath of rose blossoms against her apron. With her right, she gestures as though to drop a single rose onto the grave. Her expression is loving and serene, as if to evoke Jessie herself at the peak of her youthful innocence.

"The kindly and sympathetic face of [the] goddess looking down upon the sad scene is very impressive," the *Atwood Bee* said.

The west side of the granite column bears the Keith family's Scottish coat of arms. The face of the column includes the ineffably sad words, "We miss her at home." Elma Township is mentioned. The full inscription reads:

> JESSIE
> Born Dec. 20th 1880
> Daughter of
> Wm & Jane Keith,
> Elma.
> While defending her honor
> She lost her life
> Oct. 19th 1894.
> We miss her at home.
> Erected by her parents &
> Sympathizing friends.

The statue's unveiling took place on May 24, 1896. One and a half years had passed since the murder and one year since the hanging. An estimated three thousand people came. By chance, three days earlier, one of Listowel's most prominent and successful citizens, linseed-oil manufacturer John Livingston, had dropped dead of a heart attack at the age of sixty-two. He was buried the same day as the unveiling, and most people attended both services.

The occasion also coincided with the local Cemetery Decoration Day, still held annually in Listowel, when townsfolk decorate every grave in the graveyard with flowers. Jessie's plot was encircled with white lilies. Conducting the service was a leading secularist figure, William Algie, from the village of Alton, close to Cataract, where Chattelle was captured. Algie delivered a lengthy oration, as flowery as his surroundings and sprinkled with poetic quotations from William Shakespeare, Omar Khayyám, Robert Burns, and others. No religious controversy marred the occasion this time. As though belatedly observing William Hay's entreaties on the day of the funeral, guests focused on honouring Jessie's memory and expressing condolences to the family.

"Our assemblage here recalls the history of a young life, rudely and ruthlessly destroyed in the early morning of glad existence," Algie said to get the service under way at two o'clock. "It is unnecessary to recall the saddest day in the history of this community. The press, the telegraph, the telephone, the railway, and all the conveniences of our civilization at once lent their aid to condemn the crime and capture the criminal. I need not enumerate the scores of letters and telegrams tendering sympathy to the bereaved parents, and I am satisfied that from every home where love dwells and children play, in the length and breadth of our common country, there rose a sigh or sob of pity for the innocent victim and those who mourned her tragic and untimely death."

The speaker also paid tribute to Hay, who had died that January at sixty-four. "It is with love and respect we recall the manly voice of that brave, warm-hearted citizen, the late William G. Hay," Algie said, "whose dear remains are now at rest in this same silent city, who conducted the simple and pathetic service at the open grave."

After more poetry and extravagant oration, Algie, without naming him, made reference to the killer: "We would it were possible to avoid recalling the memory of the unhappy and unfortunate criminal who expiated his crime on the scaffold," the secularist leader said. "We must not forget that he was once 'a mother's darling,'" he continued, citing a sentimental 1869 painting of a mother and toddler called *A Mother's Darling* by English artist George Goodwin Kilburne. "[W]e do not know the whole history of the rough and thorny path of life along which he travelled from the cradle to the grave of infamy and dishonor."

Here Algie missed the mark. No evidence suggests that Chattelle was ever a mother's darling. On the contrary, in his prison memoir he said he never even knew his mother's name, an extraordinary detail. Perhaps Algie was simply trying to say that Chattelle was human, too, and not the "human fiend" or "black-hearted monster" of the newspaper stories. Or maybe he was trying to express sympathy in the spirit of "There but for the grace of God go I." The orator, however, might have done better to point out that far from being valued by his mother or father, Chattelle spent his childhood entirely cut off from parental affection and comfort. The only childhood care he received seems to have come from total strangers, including a riverboat captain, a woman who had lost her son, and a family in Saint-Damase who nursed him back to health after he fell ill. For most of his upbringing in Saint-Hyacinthe he received only abuse and rejection, and none of the nurturing a child needs to develop feelings of empathy toward oneself and others. The lovelessness of Chattelle's childhood might be the closest explanation possible for his senseless and barbaric act.

At the gravesite, Algie next turned to the grieving parents.

"To Mr. and Mrs. Keith we would say, the silent grasp of the hand and the tear-dimmed eye are the truest credentials of our sympathy," he said. "This little memorial will be a lasting testimonial of the sentiments of your friends, and as such it will be held sacred by every visitor to Fairview Cemetery."

Grief cannot be rushed, Algie said. Quoting Shakespeare, he said that when Queen Gertrude told Hamlet to "cast thy knighted colour off," Hamlet, grieving for his father, replied that his "inky cloak" was but an outer representation of a deep, abiding grief that he cannot cast off so easily.

The family needed time to grieve but time caught up to most of the Keiths. On February 26, 1898, four years after the murder and two years after the unveiling, Jessie's elder sister, Ida, died at the age of nineteen. The official cause was "phthisis," commonly called "consumption," a once common term for a wasting away of the body, often from tuberculosis. Less technically she died of heartbreak, as though Chattelle killed both sisters. "There is very little doubt," said the *Exeter Advocate*, "that her early death is to be attributed very largely to the terrible shock she received through the death of her sister Jessie under circumstances with which the whole country are only too familiar."

Ida Keith, Jessie's older sister, appears full of promise in an undated photo. The Keiths were a good-looking family.

"[Ida's] death is particularly sad," said the *Listowel Standard*, "as her decline was no doubt to a measure due to the shock and strain on her nerves through the tragic death of her sister Jessie.... The funeral on Monday was a very large one, the remains being placed by those of her murdered sister in Fairview cemetery."

A block of stone labelled simply "Ida" was placed at the foot of the Goddess of Flora and a fresh grave dug. Again William Algie officiated at the interment, again with a flowery address.

"Kind friends," he said, "standing on the soil made sacred by sad memories, and under the shadow of this memorial of sympathy, I thank you one and all for assembling today to do the last sad office that man can do for man. Words are barren and sounds are meaningless to express our sorrow for the bereaved parents, who today consign to the 'windowless place of rest' the dear remains of a loved and loving daughter."

In 1917, Jane Keith, William's wife and the mother of the three children, died at sixty-nine, also of "consumption," also attributed to the effects of the murder. "Mrs. Keith had been ailing since the time of the [Jessie Keith] tragedy," the *Listowel Banner* said.

In 1920, Alexander "Sandy" Keith, the youngest of the three children, died unmarried at thirty-four. No other information about him survives, except that he had continued to live with his father in the family home, always within sight of the rise along the railway tracks in the neighbouring field. After Sandy's death, William sold the farm and moved nearby to live with his nephew James.

William Keith lived to be almost ninety. He outlived everybody else in the family and died in 1928 of peritonitis, an abdominal infection, having enjoyed good health until then. Obituaries recalled the central tragedy of his life obliquely, perhaps because everybody already knew the details.

"Thirty-four years ago his second daughter, Jessie, was the victim of a terrible tragedy, which was a great trial," the *Banner* said, without elaborating.

After writing in his logbook, "This day Jessie was murdered," William Keith made no further entries for the rest of 1894 or part of the next year. He gave himself time to mourn, and, when he was ready, began to reengage with the world. Throughout his life, he showed a rare ability to stay true to his own values and beliefs, to live on his own terms, and at the same time associate with a broad cross-section of society. He continued to serve as secretary of the North Perth Farmers' Institute. He went on to sit as a municipal councillor and as a justice of the peace, community service roles that must have helped him reconnect.

"A man of considerable intelligence and read much," the *Monkton Times* said after his death.

His funeral was well attended. Friends and acquaintances travelled from as far away as Kitchener, Wingham, Brantford, and Clifford. To the end, he remained a freethinker, or secularist. He generally gave Christian clergymen a wide berth, but in later years often shared conversations with Reverend John Crawford, whose denomination remains unrecorded. "During his frequent visits with him they became fast friends and Mr. Crawford conducted his funeral services," the *Monkton Times* said. A Christian service would have been a betrayal, and no controversy is mentioned, suggesting that Crawford officiated for his friend in the manner of secularist leader William Hay, without prayers.

One hundred and twenty-five years later, the people of Listowel and Perth County continue to honour Jessie Keith's memory. Schoolchildren still write projects about the terrible events in the swampy wood in 1894. A few years ago, Lois Aitchison, of Stratford Memorials Ltd., in Listowel, had the memorial statue professionally cleaned of more than a century of grime at her company's expense. "You don't see the detail unless you get the moss off," she said. Visitors to Fairview Cemetery continue to seek out the Goddess of Flora, and sometimes cast fresh roses and lilies on Jessie's grave.

Part Two

CHATTELLE'S

ROUTE

THEN

AND NOW

CHAPTER 21
The Goddess of Flowers and Springtime

THE MAN WITH THE BLACK VALISE began as a chapter in a proposed book about Stratford's historic sites. The city takes pride in its built heritage and has developed a number of guided and self-guided heritage tours. Most are good at pointing out architectural details of homes and other buildings, and naming the original occupants, but the human stories behind the addresses are mostly missing. One exception is an excursion through downtown in a wagon drawn by two hefty workhorses, with Nancy Musselman usually giving the commentary.

"Have you thought of publishing your research?" I asked her at the end of one of her tours.

"I'm not a writer," she said and suggested I write something.

To interest a publisher I needed three sample chapters. I started with the first historic site on Musselman's route, the room on Ontario Street where the great American inventor Thomas Edison lived for several months as a teenage telegraph operator. After accidently causing two trains to nearly collide head-on, the boy fled the country. Not all drama in Stratford is confined to the Shakespearian stage.

Next I wrote about the Revols, a local rock band of the late 1950s and early 1960s whose individual members went on to help shape the course of North American pop music. A plaque near the Festival Theatre marks the pavilion where the group once rehearsed and performed. Lead singer and piano player Richard Manuel left to join Ronnie Hawkins and the Hawks, a group that evolved into Bob Dylan's first electric touring band and afterward found fame as the Band. Revols guitarist John Till became Janis Joplin's lead guitarist in both her Kozmic Blues Band and subsequent Full Tilt Boogie Band. Separately, both Manuel and Till performed at the seminal 1969 Woodstock music festival. Revols manager Dave Michie became radio DJ Dave Mickey and then TV and radio broadcaster David Marsden. Revols bass guitarist Ken Kalmusky joined Ian and Sylvia's Great Speckled Bird.

I needed a third sample chapter. As the landmark I picked the 1887 Perth County Court House, one of Stratford's best-loved heritage buildings, but what was the story?

"The Jessie Keith murder trial," suggested Stratford-Perth archivist Kathy Wideman, who is from Listowel. She dug out two boxes of Keith family material, including William Keith's daybook from 1894, with its chilling entry of October 19, "This day Jessie was murdered."

The more I read about the case the more I was drawn to it. People lived so differently in 1894 than we do now. They tilled fields with horses, sewed their own clothes, and kept machinery running at the mills. To get somewhere quickly they boarded a train, and to get a message out instantly they sent a telegram. Stratford produced two daily evening newspapers, and the Toronto dailies dispatched some of their best reporters to a murder story in a small Ontario town. I dropped the Stratford historic sites book to pursue *The Man with the Black Valise*.

When I get interested in a subject, I like as much as possible to experience it for myself. I like to visit physical locations. A few years ago, I started listening to African music and ended up travelling on successive trips to Senegal, Mali, Morocco, Tunisia, Kenya, Uganda, Ethiopia, and Sudan. For *The Man with the Black Valise*, I began visiting places along the route that detective John Wilson Murray mapped — the killer's trail.

Cheered by crowds lining Lakeside Drive, a bevy of swans makes its way to the water at Stratford's annual Swan Parade, held in early April as a harbinger of spring. Celebrations take place over two days.

As in Africa, a new world opened for me, or rather two worlds — one set in the nineteenth century, the other in the twenty-first.

In my modern-day travels, I stood with crowds at Stratford's Swan Parade, an early spring event in which a pipe-and-drum band leads the city's signature birds from their winter quarters to the Avon River. One summer's day, I ate my fill at Lucan Baconfest, an annual biker-friendly gathering that celebrates the hog, both the farm-animal and motorcycle kinds. I cheered contestants in the Listowel Agricultural Fair tractor pull, listened to country bands at the Stonetown Heritage Festival in St. Marys, and sampled "broasted chicken" at a destination restaurant in Millbank called Anna Mae's.

In my nineteenth-century-themed travels, I discovered Isabella and Donald McLeod's house. Or, rather, I found an old map that divided Ailsa Craig into numbered lots, and Chris Harrington, an unusually resourceful research librarian for North Middlesex County, based in Strathroy, dug up voters' lists from 1891 and 1894 that matched the numbered lots to homeowners' names. Together we nailed down current addresses. We established that the home of Gordon McEwan, the "bright young boy" who gave Chattelle the walking stick, no longer exists. Gone, too, is the home of engineer Angus McLean, who scolded Chattelle as he lay drunk on the grass. The former McLeod house, however, still stands.

Donald McLeod owned two adjacent village lots — one for the house, the other for a small barn. The barn is gone but the original McLeod residence remains, a one-and-a-half-storey home at 184 William Street, six blocks from the former North Middlesex Agricultural Fair grounds, now called Lions Park. In the Jessie Keith murder case, the building represents a key landmark — the beginning of detective John Wilson Murray's timeline and the place from which the tramp stole the black valise that directly linked him to the murder. I was excited to find the address and thrilled to see the house still standing. The people who own it today said the interior is renovated and retains no tangible connection to nineteenth-century life, but they had no objection to my publishing the location.

The house originally belonging to Donald and Isabella McLeod still stands at 184 William Street in Ailsa Craig. On October 3, 1894, Amédée Chattelle entered through a window and stole women's clothing and the black valise.

Part two of *The Man with the Black Valise* recounts my many discoveries along the killer's route of 1894. The section adds to the Jessie Keith murder narrative in the way bonus material often adds to a podcast. I got the idea for part two while listening to *Cocaine and Rhinestones*, a podcast on the history of country music, by Tyler Mahan Coe. On his website, Coe displays covers of the books he researched, posts a transcript of each episode, and adds information that he forgot to include while recording the podcast. Other podcast websites go further. *Serial*, Sarah Koenig's seminal true-crime podcast, uses its webpages to post photos, graphics, maps, letters, timelines, written sidebars, and animated art.

On podcast websites, the connection between the audio narrative and the bonus material usually needs no explanation. Here, the relationship between the Jessie Keith murder case and the part two stories is not always as direct. Part two flowed from my research on the case, not always from the case itself, and the research sometimes took me on tangents. As I physically traced Amédée Chattelle's route through Middlesex, Perth, and Wellington Counties, heritage landmarks would stand out for me, and I would get drawn to the human stories behind the addresses.

In Ailsa Craig, in addition to finding the McLeod house, I heard how sixteen-year-old Kathleen McIntyre saved the village from a conflagration and was rewarded with a gold medallion. In Lucan, I visited the sites connected to the so-called Black Donnellys, and a period of violent anarchy that stands in stark contrast to the sense of orderly justice shared by the people of Listowel, in the next county. In St. Marys, I walked into the same downtown buildings where Chattelle shopped for his brown-striped cottonade overalls and the razor-sharp I*XL jackknife that he used as a murder weapon.

East of Stratford, I stopped at Fryfogel's Tavern, a little off Chattelle's route but a key Perth County historic site — the place where the county's first white settler, Sebastian Fryfogel, built the first stagecoach stop on the Huron Road. In nearby Baden, I attended an evening folk concert on the lawn of Castle Kilbride, a museum and national historic site with a connection to Listowel's John Livingston, buried the same day that the Goddess of Flora statue was unveiled.

In Stratford, I toured the Perth County Court House, my original starting point for the book, where Chattelle was tried and convicted of Jessie's murder. I found coroner James Rankin's house on Erie Street and learned of a tragedy in his own family, and I viewed the plaque on Ontario Street commemorating police chief John McCarthy's premature death by fire, a tragedy for the entire city.

Chattelle was the first convicted murderer hanged in Perth County, but two others followed in 1909 and 1954. I studied both cases. North of Stratford, I followed Chattelle's route past Millbank and Newton. I walked to the rise of land past the former Keith farm to the spot where Chattelle first encountered Jessie on the tracks, and I followed his path out of town. One weekend I cycled the Elora Cataract Trailway. Now a recreational trail along the old rail line, it includes the last forty-five kilometres of Chattelle's escape route to Cataract. On the trip, I stopped at another national historic site, the former House of Industry and Refuge, or "poorhouse," which Chattelle would have passed on the tracks.

With this book, I wish both to help perpetuate the memory of young Jessie Keith and to share my fondness for the historic sites of Middlesex, Perth, and Wellington Counties. I have one other, overriding, ambition for the book. I wish to draw attention to the Goddess of Flora statue at Jessie's — and her sister Ida's — grave in Fairview Cemetery, Listowel. It is an extraordinary piece of sculpture, a figure of sweet tenderness commemorating one of the ugliest moments in Perth County history.

To me, the statue symbolizes the humanity of the people of Listowel and Perth County. As appalling as Jessie's death was, order at least prevailed. The social and justice systems worked. There was no wrongful conviction, no police foul-up, no lawyer getting the killer off on a technicality, and no mob lynching. Instead, Crown attorney John Idington disseminated a "Wanted" bulletin. Detective Murray scoured the countryside for witnesses and developed a map and timeline. Train station attendant William Travis apprehended the suspect. Police chief John McCarthy and his officers jailed him, and John Douglas Armour, chief justice of the Ontario Court of Queen's Bench, hands trembling, delivered the most appropriate sentence under the circumstances: death by hanging. Jessie's murder and mutilation unleashed uncertainty and chaos, but the responsible behaviour of the authorities and the general decency of the citizenry helped ensure justice for the criminal and the restoration of social order.

The statue is beginning to deteriorate. Sculptors appreciate Carrara marble partly for its softness, a characteristic that also leaves it vulnerable to the elements. The Goddess of Flora's right hand, which extends as though to cast a rose on Jessie's grave, is starting to resemble melted wax. Her face, while continuing to express its original, gentle beauty, similarly shows signs of weathering. In Florence, Italy, art preservationists moved Michelangelo's *David* indoors to the Galleria dell'Accademia from the Piazza della Signoria. In Perth County, maybe the guardians of local heritage will do the same for the Goddess of Flora. I am in the process of working with others to have the monument recognized by the Ontario Heritage Trust as an Ontario Historic Site.

At some point in every episode of *Cocaine and Rhinestones*, Tyler Mahan Coe asks his listeners, to tell one person about the podcast. Tell your followers on Facebook and Twitter if you like, he says, but also personally tell one person who would likely be interested. I suggest the same for the reader of this book. Maybe you know somebody who reads true crime. Tell that person about *The Man with the Black Valise*. Maybe you know somebody who likes to visit small museums, or national historic sites, or who generally takes an interest in nineteenth-century Ontario. Or maybe you know a theatregoer who attends the Stratford Festival, which runs from mid-April to early November and attracts half a million visitors a year. Fifty kilometres from Stratford's Festival Theatre stands the Goddess of Flora. For theatre patrons wishing to explore a bit of their surroundings between plays, the site makes an easy drive. My hope is that, through this book, travellers from far and wide will learn about the story behind the graveyard memorial and want to view it.

CHAPTER 22
Ailsa Craig: Teenage Hero

RON WALKER STOPS HIS CAR at the last house in the village's
north end. He is a robust, cheerful man, who traces both sides of his
family six generations to Ailsa Craig's early days. He is also president of the
Ailsa Craig and District Historical Society, making him the ideal guide to
offer a special heritage tour. The house is our first stop. It is a two-storey
Georgian home built in 1864 of local yellow brick. A plaque out front
shows a portrait of a well-dressed gentleman with enormous side whiskers,
the area's earliest white settler, David Craig.

"Mr. Craig came here from New York," Walker says. "He was an
engineer who had spent a lot of time travelling between New York and
Boston, and I've also found accounts of him sailing to Cuba, where he
built large refining machines for sugar plantations. Obviously he was well
heeled. I often think of his poor wife, Janet, who would have left quite a
noble life to come literally to the bush. From here you can't see the river
flats very well, but they formed an area rich in deer, as well as wolves and
bears, and in the summertime the Seneca would come up from New York
State to hunt them. By all accounts, Mrs. Craig lived here for nine months
before she saw another white person."

David and Janet Craig first arrived in Upper Canada in the mid-1830s from New York and built a log cabin on the embankment overlooking the Ausable River. In 1858, to encourage railway builders, David donated a parcel of land for a station and asked that it be called "Craig's Station." When he discovered the name already taken, he cleverly chose "Ailsa Craig," preserving his surname "Craig" while paying tribute to the Scottish island of Ailsa Craig on the Firth of Clyde, visible from his boyhood home.

Craig's pioneering efforts set the village on a course to prosperity that, ultimately, he himself failed to enjoy. "Old Mr. Craig died penniless and an alcoholic," Walker says unsentimentally. "His son got involved in horse racing and spent all his dad's money, a tragic end."

At the south edge of town, we stop at a grand-looking estate with a gravel drive curving around mature trees and well-tended gardens. At the end stands a house of painted white brick, two and a half storeys high, with a front porch running the length of the building, a picture of nineteenth-century charm.

Ron Walker stands in front of the beautifully preserved former Falstaff Hotel and Tavern, one of five hotels built in the village after the railroad made it an important cattle-shipment centre. The structure, at Church and John Streets, is now a private home.

"William Shipley's place," Walker says. "Ailsa Craig has two founding fathers. Shipley is the other one."

While Craig owned the land north of what is now Main Street, or Highway 7, Shipley, an Englishman who arrived in the 1860s, acquired the land south of the road. By then, a small logging settlement had sprung up. Pursuing mutual ambitions, Craig and Shipley laid out a village site and carved up some of their lands to sell as lots. Craig also donated property for Anglican and Presbyterian churches, Shipley for Baptist and Methodist ones. The churches and land deeds attracted more settlers, and, by the time the village was incorporated in 1874, Ailsa Craig was thriving as a regional farming, commercial, and cattle-trading centre. Just as tragedy touched the Craigs, however, it also touched the Shipleys.

"They had two sons and a daughter," Walker says of William Shipley and his wife, Mary. "Neither son married and his daughter he virtually sold."

By the late 1890s, for reasons lost to history, Shipley was close to bankruptcy. His chances appeared to improve only when he met a newly arrived Englishman, Edward Rawlinson, who offered to pay Shipley's debts in return for the hand of his daughter, Annie Ada. Rawlinson professed love for her but she rebuffed his affections. He was twenty-two, she twenty-five. Although beautiful, she was also fragile.

"There was a tennis court on the Shipley lawn and all the young people of the village used to go there to enjoy the game," local historian Janet Morton Cree writes in *Ailsa Craig, Ontario, Canada: Centennial 1874–1974*. "For many weeks at a time, Miss Ada was confined to her bed, but was allowed to sit up and watch the young people. Before they left for home, they would gather round her window for a visit. It was noticeable that she spurned Mr. Rawlinson each time he appeared in the group."

Eventually, the desperate father and ardent suitor struck a deal. On the morning of Tuesday, November 15, 1898, news went around the village that Edward Rawlinson and Annie Ada Shipley were to marry at the Shipley home that morning at eleven o'clock. Afterward they were to board the three o'clock train to Toronto for their honeymoon. Well-wishers flocked to the station to see them off, Cree writes, "although a few nobler souls stayed at home, feeling that they could not endure the sorrow of a forced marriage."

Founding fathers William Shipley, left, and David Craig take pride of place in a mural on the side of Ailsa Craig's nineteenth-century general store, also pictured in the upper right. The public school and Odd Fellows Hall are gone. The 1906 Town Hall survived the 1923 fire and currently serves as an arts centre. Temperance House, built after the fire, now houses the Foodland supermarket.

A few days later, Annie Ada was found dead in Toronto at the Queen's Hotel. No record of the cause of death can be found, and contemporary local newspapers were silent on the matter. The plaque in front of the Shipley home suggests she died of heart failure.

"She might have poisoned herself," Walker says in his cheerful, un-sugar-coated way.

The theme of our tour is nineteenth-century Ailsa Craig, but Walker pulls over at the corner of Main and John Streets to tell me about the village's worst twentieth-century disaster and its greatest hero.

"We lost everything between this red house near the corner to the Town Hall and the entire block opposite," he says. "It doesn't seem like a big expanse but it decimated the town. In early May, it would have been getting dark by about six, the electricity was out, and the downtown was on fire. You can imagine the horror."

On Monday, May 7, 1923, at 3:45 in the afternoon, eight-year-old Jimmy Dodds smelled smoke on his way home from school. It was coming from a shed behind the White & May dry-goods store. The boy ran to alert the town constable, James Priestly, who hurried over to ring the Town Hall bell. By then the adjacent Brodie barn had also caught fire.

"Soon the town was in an uproar," the *London Free Press* reported. "Bells were clanging and for a time a near panic held sway."

The chief of the volunteer fire department, Alex Findlay, led the emergency response. Villagers took turns at old-fashioned hand-pumps attached to fire hydrants and a network of hoses. Volunteers also ran five hundred metres of hose from the railway's water tower to the blaze, and when the tower's supply ran out they formed bucket brigades — long lines of men passing pails of water from hand to hand from the Ausable River.

At the Bell Telephone exchange, in a building that was also burning, sixteen-year-old Kathleen McIntyre coolly placed emergency calls. She was the sole operator on duty. She rang firefighters in surrounding municipalities — Parkhill, Lucan, Crediton, and Dashwood — and summoned the London fire department, which for the first time in its history dispatched a fire truck outside its municipal boundaries.

"Chief [John] Aitken, with his men, made a record run, doing the 25 odd miles in 35 minutes," the *Free Press* said of the rush to the scene, an average of seventy kilometres an hour.

McIntyre also reached individual farmers. Abandoning all other work, they arrived by the hundred. When it became clear that larger volumes of water were needed, she called the railway to stop its trains until workers could dig under the tracks and run hoses directly from the river.

A spring breeze blew up, casting cinders over the village. The roof of the Anglican rectory caught fire but responders put it out. At the Town Hall, James McKay climbed to the roof and doused burning embers with water that he hauled in pails from below, saving that building as well.

"At one time it looked as if the whole village would go up in smoke and women for several blocks around cleared their homes of all belongings," the *Free Press* said. "Furniture and bedding were strewn along the streets and men and women with blankets climbed to the roofs and fought the incipient flames."

When burning hydro poles started falling, operator McIntyre tried desperately to reach the hydroelectric distribution station, and, when nobody answered, she tracked down Lilly Yelf, wife of the local hydro employee, who pulled a large switch to cut all electrical power to the village. The only remaining light came from oil lamps and the inferno itself. By that point, the windows of the Bell Telephone building were cracking, and McIntyre noticed that her cheeks were getting hot. Without electricity, her work was finished anyway, and she fled the office just before it collapsed.

Nobody died in the fire. The only casualties were Duncan Campbell, who badly burned his hand, and a dog belonging to Joseph Middaugh, owner of a grocery that burned down. The grocer had carried the pet from the store, but for some reason the dog returned inside and was never seen again.

Perhaps the most touching moment came with the rescue of Dorothy and Ila Clarke, daughters of the owners of a harness shop lost to the blaze.

"These two little kiddies were in bed in their home over the store when the flames reached the building and they had to be carried out," the *Free Press* said. "Dorothy, who is only 11 years of age, fell off her bicycle some time ago and was paralysed, she has not walked since. Ila, her sister, is about 13 … a victim of heart trouble and also … confined to her bed. The children cried bitterly as they were carried from the burning building."

Material losses were staggering. George Meadow's red-brick house near the corner of John Street was saved, but five other families were left homeless, including those living above or behind their shops. The main businesses destroyed included the White & May dry-goods store, the Clarke saddle and harness shop, Middaugh's grocery, the Bell Telephone exchange, two boot-and-shoe stores, a farm-implement agency, a seed store, a general store, and the village skating rink.

Of all the heroes of the day, teenaged McIntyre stood out.

"Real heroism should not go unrecognized," the *London Free Press* said on Wednesday, two days after the fire. "Despite dense volumes of smoke, falling glass and almost unbearable heat, Miss McIntyre stayed at the phone switchboard."

"I was in no danger at all," the girl said modestly.

The ten-karat-gold medal, presented to teenaged telephone operator Kathleen McIntyre for her heroism in the 1923 fire, constitutes the most prized object of the Ailsa Craig and District Historical Society. The society displays a replica at its museum and keeps this original locked in a safe.

"Every man, woman and child in the village," the paper said, "asserts that if it had not been for her bravery the entire village would have been wiped off the map and the conflagration might have exacted a heavy toll of lives. To give Miss McIntyre a medal in recognition of her bravery is a mere trifle to what the young lady deserves."

The newspaper cast a ten-karat-gold medal the size of a modern Canadian quarter, and attached it to a gold chain. "A tribute to the heroic work of Miss Kathleen McIntyre at the Ailsa Craig fire May 7th, 1923," says the inscription on one side. "Presented by the London Free Press," says the reverse.

Three days after the fire, well-wishers filled London's Allen Theatre to capacity. London's populist mayor and former stunt-bicycle rider George Wenige presided, along with officials from other municipalities and the Bell Telephone Company.

"They struck that medal and presented it to her," Walker says. "Today we'd still be fighting three months later about what the medal was going to look like and whether to serve cake and coffee."

Late in life, McIntyre bequeathed the medal to the Ailsa Craig and District Historical Society. The group understood its value. Walker had it duplicated for display and keeps the original locked in a safe.

AILSA CRAIG QUILT AND FIBRE ARTS FESTIVAL

The high point of the Ailsa Craig calendar today is a May festival celebrating the quilting and fibre arts of other countries, a different one each year. Two hundred volunteers cook food and put up displays. Supporters donate money to fly nine or ten quilters from the honoured country and pay them for talks and lectures. Residents open their homes as accommodation for the speakers.

"In an urban area you will often see quilts being discarded at a garage sale," says festival chair Shelagh Morrison. "In this community they are treasured."

Countries featured so far include Russia, Ireland, Great Britain, France, Israel, Denmark, Holland, Latvia, Iceland, New Zealand, and several African nations collectively. To commemorate each festival edition, volunteers paint one quilt design each year to mount along a paved trail through local Lions Park, the former grounds of the North Middlesex Agricultural Fair, which Amédée Chattelle visited in 1894.

Visitors to the 2018 Ailsa Craig Quilt and Fibre Arts Festival examine pieces from the year's featured country, Iceland. Every year, the village comes together to celebrate quilts and textile arts with displays and lectures.

CHAPTER 23
Lucan: Mass Murder of the Black Donnellys

PULP CRIME WRITER Thomas P. Kelley kicked off a Canadian literary subgenre with his 1953 nonfiction thriller, *The Black Donnellys*. It depicted a family of Irish immigrant psychopaths who helped open what is now the flat, fertile, farm country around Lucan, Ontario, while terrorizing their neighbours. The Donnellys burned barns and sheds, sawed carriages in half, mutilated farm animals, stole produce for resale, and in hotel bars on Saturday nights beat up whomever they pleased. To end the outrage, Kelley wrote, some thirty of the good citizens of Biddulph Township, on a cold winter's night in 1880, murdered five of the Donnelly family — two of whom were women — and their dog. Two trials were held. Both juries acquitted the accused killers and the town celebrated.

The Black Donnellys is said to have sold four hundred thousand copies in its first twenty years, breaking the silence on a vigilante mass murder that Lucan had been trying to keep quiet for decades. Even though Kelley sided with the villagers, local residents resented the book. They preferred not to be known for anarchy and cold-blooded murder. Some also challenged Kelley's facts. While the author said he researched newspaper files and court records, he also called himself "king of the Canadian pulp writers," admitting a taste for sensationalism and a casual regard for accuracy. His treatment seemed to cry out for a more objective account, and nonfiction authors, novelists, playwrights, magazine journalists, and singer-songwriters have been revising the narrative ever since.

The first to challenge Kelley was Orlo Miller, in 1962. A former newspaper reporter and later an ordained Anglican minister, he wrote *The Donnellys Must Die*, a sometimes-sanctimonious account arguing that the Donnellys might have been bad, but not bad enough to be slaughtered. "There is no question that upon occasion the members of the Donnelly family committed misdemeanours," Miller wrote in his plodding style. "There can equally be no question that they did not merit the savage punishment meted out to them by their neighbours."

The rewrite satisfied nobody. That same year, Kelley reworked his material into a novel, *Vengeance of the Black Donnellys: Canada's Most Feared Family Strikes Back from the Grave*. Miller answered with his own novel, *Death to the Donnellys*. York University professor Norman N. Feltes wrote a nonfiction treatise, *This Side of Heaven*, attempting to illuminate the story using what he called "rigorous Marxist structuralist methodology." *Toronto Star* reporter Peter Edwards wrote *Night Justice: The True Story of the Black Donnellys*, making the surprising claim that vigilante justice was once "all too common in small communities." Playwright James Reaney of London, Ontario, wrote a trilogy of overlapping works, which he collectively titled *The Donnellys* and which his publisher said "elevated the events to the level of legend."

The most ambitious reckoning came in 1995 with a catalogue-sized tome by Hamilton lawyer Ray Fazakas, called *The Donnelly Album: The Complete & Authentic Account of Canada's Famous Feuding Family*. "Complete" turned out to be an overstatement. Fazakas followed with three more books: *In Search of the Donnellys* (2001), *In Search of the Donnellys: Revised Edition* (2006), and *In Search of the Donnellys: Second Revised Edition* (2012).

Musicians also reworked the material. In 1970, barn-dance star Earl Heywood released an album of fourteen songs, *Tales of the Donnelly Feud*.

That same year, singer-songwriter Gene MacLellan recorded "Death of the Black Donnellys" along with his more famous song, "Snowbird," a *Billboard* No. 1 hit for Anne Murray. Also in the early 1970s, folk hero Stompin' Tom Connors recorded "Black Donnelly's Massacre," with a misplaced apostrophe, and "Jenny Donnelly," honouring the youngest Donnelly child. A number of regional singers added to the canon, and in 2002 major U.S. recording artist Steve Earle released "Justice in Ontario," awkwardly rhyming "from Ontario" with "the Donnellys Oh."

A slew of moviemakers turned out films and shows. In 2007, NBC aired *The Black Donnellys*, a TV drama series that referenced the Lucan Donnellys but actually revolved around four fictional Irish American brothers in New York. Ten years later, independent Canadian filmmaker Aaron Huggett released a forty-five-minute docudrama about the Lucan events using Kelley's original title, *The Black Donnellys*.

The books, songs, plays, and movies keep coming. At last count, the Donnelly catalogue numbered seventeen nonfiction works, six novels, three plays, a plethora of recordings, and numerous dramatic and documentary films of various lengths. Despite the output, however, the Donnelly story has never truly taken root in the Canadian consciousness. It has failed to resonate in Canadian culture. One explanation could be that the drama runs counter to Canada's self-image as a country of "peace, order and good government." Another reason might be that the story has no hero. Everybody is nasty.

Kelley was not exaggerating when he said that in the middle of the night, in cold blood, some thirty local men murdered five Donnelly family members, including two women, and their dog. A far greater number of people knew of the conspiracy in advance and none tried to stop it. In fact, the bloodbath was led by the local police constable. As author Ray Fazakas makes clear, a great many Irish Catholic immigrants to Lucan, not just the Donnellys, brought with them a feud mentality rooted in the rural villages of Tipperary County, Ireland. Their disputes were not Catholic versus Protestant; everybody was Catholic. Their grudges were not even clan versus clan. The Tipperary immigrants were simply trapped in a rowdy, destructive, anti-social way of life that pitted neighbour against neighbour in an ongoing series of retributions, reprisals, retaliations, and paybacks. They proved themselves the antithesis of the Scottish and Irish immigrants of Listowel, in neighbouring Perth County, who so properly brought Amédée Chattelle to justice.

If an arrest were attempted in Lucan, the arresting officer would be bullied and sometimes shot at. None stayed long on the job. If criminal charges were laid, witnesses would be frightened into silence and judges intimidated into leniency. No police chief, no Crown attorney, no court justice, no politician, no authority of any kind went to the rescue of a village sinking deeper and deeper into dysfunction. Although Provincial Police detective John Wilson Murray had started his job in 1875, his bosses similarly failed to assign him either to several earlier unsolved killings in the area or to the mass murder itself.

As outside the mainstream consciousness as the story is, however, a steady trickle of curiosity seekers arrives in Lucan every summer to visit the Donnelly sites. Rather than discourage such visitors, the town embraces them. In 2009, with the support of then-mayor Tom McLaughlin and his council, the Lucan Area Heritage and Donnelly Museum opened on Main Street.

The Lucan Area Heritage and Donnelly Museum avoids the term *Black Donnellys* as unnecessarily pejorative, but colours its logo predominantly black. Featured are, left to right, brothers Robert, Will, and Michael.

"Certainly, some of my ancestors, even my parents, would be surprised that I support talk about this type of thing," the former mayor says at the museum, where he works as a volunteer. "[The Donnelly killings] used to be our biggest secret."

McLaughlin is the descendant of one of the accused vigilantes. His great-grandfather's brother, Martin McLaughlin, went on trial for the Donnelly murders, accused specifically of shooting and killing John Donnelly. Martin had arrived in the township as a child, grew to become a successful farmer, and shortly before the murders was named a Middlesex County justice of the peace.

"A pillar of the community," his descendant says. "I don't see him going to the Donnelly homestead with the intent to kill.… I think most of them wanted to go there and say 'This is going to stop.'"

McLaughlin says he has read all the Donnelly books. Ray Fazakas has done the best job, he says, but even the Fazakas books cannot be fully relied upon. "There's only one way to get the story straight," the former mayor says, "and that is to go down to St. Patrick's cemetery, dig up certain people, bring them back to life, and get them to tell the truth."

THE DONNELLY STORY

The first thing a visitor learns about the Donnelly story is that it covers hundreds of quarrels spread over more than twenty years. The year 1857 can be said to be Year One of the trouble. James Donnelly Sr. and his wife, Johannah, were living in a log cabin eight kilometres northeast of Lucan on the Roman Line, a concession road named for the Irish Roman Catholic settlers. James Sr. and Johannah had seven sons. A daughter would come later. James Sr. was engaged in an ongoing dispute with his neighbour, Patrick Farrell, and at a neighbourhood logging bee Donnelly killed Farrell in a fight.

The single comical episode came next. Rather than turn himself in, James Sr. hid in the woods near his home for nearly a year, sometimes dressing in his wife's clothes to work in the fields. Finally fed up with fugitive living, he had a friend turn him in on the understanding that he and the friend would split the reward. Nobody was fooled, however, and no reward was paid. At trial, James Sr. was condemned to hang, but the sentence was later commuted to seven years in prison. John A. Macdonald, Canada's future first prime minister, signed the commutation papers as attorney general of Upper Canada.

Shortly after James Sr.'s imprisonment, daughter Jenny was born. For seven years, Johannah raised eight children as a single mother. In 1865, James Sr. returned to a household that included seven strapping boys: James Jr., Will, John, Patrick, Michael, Robert, and Thomas. To defend the family name against schoolyard taunts, they had learned to retaliate with their fists.

Low-level troublemaking began. Arrests for larceny were contested and acquittals won. In 1871, the Donnelly brothers aggressively entered the stagecoach business, competing fiercely with rival companies and precipitating years of violent conflict that saw coaches sabotaged, stables go up in flames, and horses burned alive. One outrage followed another. By the time the stagecoach business declined with the coming of the London, Huron and Bruce Railway in 1878, retributive violence had become commonplace throughout the county, with barn burnings, animal mutilations, threats of lynching, and the occasional unsolved murder. The Donnellys were often to blame, and they were often accused whether they were to blame or not.

"There was a reign of terror [in 1875]," County of Middlesex Crown attorney Charles Hutchison wrote in a contemporary account. "No one dare go against the Donnellys."

"Unchecked rowdyism ... is hurting the village," the *Exeter Times* said in 1876.

"A gloom of a most appalling nature is gradually settling down on the inhabitants of unhappy Lucan," the *London Daily Advertiser* reported in 1877 during a wave of arsons.

"The welfare of the place has of late been imperilled by the unfortunate exhibitions of malice," the *Illustrated Historical Atlas of the County of Middlesex* said in 1878.

In the early hours of February 4, 1880, the violence peaked with the Donnelly murders. Thirty men, carrying clubs and calling themselves the Vigilance Committee, left their meeting place at the Cedar Swamp Schoolhouse and walked more than four kilometres across the snow-packed fields to the Donnelly homestead. They arrived at one in the morning. Their alleged ringleader, the recently appointed police constable, James Carroll, opened the unlocked kitchen door and handcuffed Tom Donnelly, the youngest son, in his bed. "You're under arrest," Carroll said.

Four others were also asleep in their beds: James Sr., and his wife, Johannah, both in their sixties; their niece Bridget, twenty-two, and a neighbour's boy, eleven-year-old Johnny O'Connor. On a signal from Constable Carroll, the vigilantes stormed the house.

When Tom, still handcuffed, tried to run, somebody levelled him with a pitchfork in the back. He was dragged back into the house, where the mob beat him to death with clubs and shovels. The vigilantes also beat James Sr. and Johannah to death. Bridget ran upstairs, and one of the men followed her and killed her. When James Sr.'s little dog wouldn't stop barking, somebody chopped off its head with an axe. A more sadistic attack on a family can scarcely be imagined. Young Johnny O'Connor saved himself by hiding under a bed, and when the mob poured burning lamp oil on the mattresses, setting the house on fire, he scrambled over the Donnelly bodies and escaped unnoticed through the flames.

Afterward, most of the vigilantes proceeded to nearby Whelan's Corners. Will, the second son and the most hated of the Donnellys, lived there with his wife, Nora. The killers entered the barn and tortured Will's prize stallion, intending to rouse the household with the horse's screams. When one of the gang opened the door of the house, two of them, allegedly including Martin McLaughlin, shot him in the throat and chest. They thought they were shooting Will but instead killed his visiting brother, John, the third and least offensive son.

Five Donnellys lay dead at two Donnelly farms. The next day, survivors Johnny O'Connor and Will Donnelly identified many of the vigilantes to police, and more than a dozen men were arrested. Six stood trial, including alleged ringleader police constable James Carroll. None was convicted.

"Stronger evidence, both direct and circumstantial, has rarely been brought against any man who in the face of it escaped the gallows," the *Toronto Globe* said of Carroll. For the Donnellys, justice was denied.

HISTORIC TOUR OF LUCAN AND BIDDULPH COUNTY

Joseph Hall's Farm

Whether Amédée Chattelle knew of the Donnelly murders when he stopped in Lucan is not recorded. Joseph Hall, the farmer who hired him to dig a well, makes no appearance in the Donnelly narratives, nor do any other Halls. Steve Earle's song mentions a "Corporal Terry Hall" in his song, "Justice in Ontario," but Earle is singing about two unrelated cases — the Donnelly slaughter of 1880 and the killing of outlaw biker Bill Matiyek at Port Hope in 1978. OPP Corporal Terry Hall investigated the Port Hope case.

Through documentation in the museum archives, former mayor McLaughlin established Joseph Hall's farm to have stretched from the east end of town, south of the railway tracks. The tracks ran immediately south of and parallel to William Street, meaning almost in front of postmaster William Porte's former property. As William Street continues east across Main Street, it becomes Alice Street, named after William Porte's daughter. It ends at Saintsbury Line, the eastern edge of Lucan. Hall's farm would have started there and run south of the tracks, meaning Chattelle could have met Hall while walking along the tracks toward St. Marys. The land was recently developed for new housing.

John Coursey, who lost the dance contest to Hall in 1888, could be the same John Coursey who in the Donnelly books appears briefly as a Lucan police constable. In 1876, in the barroom of the Revere House, Constable Coursey attempted to arrest the eldest of the seven Donnelly brothers, James Jr., for beating up one-armed Rhody Kennedy. James complied with the arrest, but his brother Will Donnelly threatened to shoot Coursey, and Coursey released James. Will was later charged for threatening Coursey but at trial was acquitted. The Revere House has since been demolished.

Lucan Area Heritage and Donnelly Museum

The museum at 171 Main Street stands on the site of the former Central Hotel, the oldest of Lucan's seven early hotels, destroyed by fire in 1995.

Thomas P. Kelley's Smith-Corona Silent Deluxe portable typewriter sits in a glass case at the Lucan Area Heritage and Donnelly Museum, surrounded by Donnelly family photos and other materials related to the 1880 mass murder. Kelley broke the silence on the vigilante killings with his 1953 bestseller, *The Black Donnellys*.

A short film detailing the Donnelly story is fleshed out with displays of family photos, court dockets, and period artifacts. Much of the collection comes from fifty years of sleuthing by lawyer and author Ray Fazakas. A replica tombstone listing the five murder victims comes from a CBC TV production. A replica stagecoach comes from a 2002 outdoor theatre production at the nearby Blythe Festival. Elsewhere on the property, period log cabins from the area illustrate 1880 settlement living.

Queen's Hotel

Now home to Lucan Drug Mart, the building at 180 Main Street originated in the 1850s as the Queen's Hotel. Patrick Flanagan's stagecoach company, an archrival to the Donnelly firm, stabled his horses and parked his coaches behind the hotel, accessible by the passageway that can still be seen through the adjacent building. In 1875, the Flanagan stables went up in flames. Two of the Donnelly brothers were suspected. No charges were laid.

Bikers arriving for Baconfest 2018 ride past Lucan Drug Mart, the former 1850s Queen's Hotel, behind which Donnelly rival Patrick Flanagan parked his horses and stagecoaches via the adjacent passageway. The annual July festival celebrating hogs helps maintain the town's outlaw image.

William Porte's Post Office

In 1888, Lucan's first postmaster, William Porte, relocated to the north-west corner of Main and William Streets. In 1908, he replaced his frame house and office with the unusual wedge-shaped red-brick building that still stands. Over the years, Porte remained on good terms with the Donnellys. He also kept a daybook in which he often recorded the weather and various goings-on. In 2009, the journals were published as *Passing into Oblivion: The Diaries of William Porte, Lucan, Ontario, 1864–1898*.

McIlhargy Tavern

There is no street number, but at the south end of town, just past a Tim Hortons and a chiropractic clinic, stands one of Lucan's earliest landmarks. It is the former McIlhargy Tavern, built by Patrick McIlhargy between 1845 and 1850 from hand-made clay bricks. The barroom, since demolished, extended south from the dining room (the limit of its foundations can still be seen). The upstairs ballroom sometimes served as a courtroom where over the years various Donnellys made appearances.

St. Patrick's Roman Catholic Church and Graveyard

If you drive two and a half kilometres past Tim Hortons out of town, on Highway 4, you will reach the Roman Line, with St. Patrick's Church on the corner. The Donnelly funeral took place here on Friday, February 6, 1880. Two caskets lay near the altar, one holding John's body, the other containing the charred remains of James Sr., Johannah, Tom, and Bridget. During his sermon, Father John Connelly stopped and "wept like a child for several minutes," Fazarkas says in *The Donnelly Album*. The common grave of the five murdered Donnellys can be found by following the churchyard's central laneway to the end and veering left a short distance across the grass. "Farewell we meet no more on this side of heaven," the inscription reads. The original marker, similar to the replica at the museum, also had the word *murdered* etched into it below each name. Souvenir hunters chipped pieces from the stone until church authorities got fed up and removed it in 1964. Donnelly descendants replaced it with a more modest gravestone, but visitors still chip off pieces as souvenirs.

The stone marking the common grave of the five murdered Donnellys in St. Patrick's churchyard bears evidence of damage from souvenir hunters. An original, more elaborate, monument was replaced in 1964 because visitors similarly chipped away at it.

The Cedar Swamp Schoolhouse

Northeast of the church, at the corner of Highway 23 (Mitchell Line) and Fallon Drive, stands the picturesque brick schoolhouse where the vigilantes held meetings in early 1880, including their final assembly on the night of the murders. Former mayor Tom McLaughlin says he attended the school as a child. It was abandoned in the 1960s and is falling into ruin.

The Donnelly Homestead

At 34937 Roman Line, large, flat fieldstones can still be seen at what would have been the corners of the home the Donnelly family built in 1870. The stones raised the house slightly to keep it from rotting. Rob Salts, a former schoolteacher who, with his wife, Linda, now owns the property, gives guided tours of the massacre site. He walked me through every detail, from the moment James Sr. and Johannah arrived on the Roman Line in 1847, to the moment young Johnny O'Connor ran from the flaming house over their bodies. "Let me show you where the bodies

Robert Donnelly, left, sixth child in the infamous family, stands with his nephew James Donnelly, son of Michael, the fifth child, in front of a house moved to the original Donnelly family homestead after the 1880 murders and fire. The home, with additions to the front and back, now serves as Rob and Linda Salts's residence.

were found," Salts said. He showed me where Tom had been handcuffed, where James Sr. had been sleeping, where Johannah fell, where Bridget ran upstairs, and where Johnny hid under the bed.

One year after the murders, in 1881, Will Donnelly purchased a house from a neighbouring farm and, with horses and logs, rolled it to a spot beside the charred ruins of his parents' home. The replacement still stands, sandwiched between additions built in 1971. The Salts live in the combined building. The Donnelly barn, built after the murders in about 1900, also still stands, reinforced by a modern concrete foundation. During his tours, Rob Salts, a self-described clairvoyant, talks of his encounters with the Donnelly ghosts.

CHAPTER 24
St. Marys: Amédée Chattelle Goes Shopping

ST. MARYS CALLS ITSELF "Stonetown" for its historic limestone quarries and the buildings they produced. Every summer, the town holds the Stonetown Heritage Festival to celebrate the landmark structures, especially those along downtown Queen Street East where Amédée Chattelle came to shop and get a haircut. On October 15, 1894, he arrived in fine weather wearing a stiff-brimmed Christy hat and carrying five dollars in his pocket.

First, he bought a pair of black, laced shoes with toecaps. Several shoe and boot shops existed at the time, and there is no way now to establish where he made the purchase. The rest of his route, however, can be traced. Amy Cubberley, chief curator and archivist at the St. Marys Museum and Archives, helped me sift through card files and newspaper microfilm to establish the tramp's progress through town.

At noon, he entered Crozier's Barber Shop, which in 1894 stood at Queen and Water Streets, in a frame building that has since burned down.

After getting a haircut and shave, and lingering to socialize, Chattelle proceeded to A.H. Lofft & Co., where he bought the grey cottonade

Hometown boy Darcy John, in the white T-shirt, far right, headlines the Saturday evening Stonetown Heritage Festival street party in 2018 on Queen Street East. Born and raised in St. Marys, John found success in Nashville as a lead guitarist for touring country music acts and as frontman in his own band.

To walk through the doorway of today's Four Happy Restaurant is to walk through the entrance that Amédée Chattelle would have used when the building housed A.H. Lofft & Co. He bought the pair of overalls that were later found in the valise at the murder scene.

The Canadian Baseball Hall of Fame and Museum offices occupy the middle unit of the historic Guest Block at 140 Queen Street East. In 1894, the unit housed J.C. Gilpin's hardware store, where Amédée Chattelle bought his murder weapon.

overalls with brown stripes that were later found bloodstained in the black valise at the murder scene. Sales clerk William Rogers wrote a receipt, later found in one of Chattelle's pockets on his arrest. The former A.H. Lofft & Co. building stood one block east of the barbershop, identifiable today as 139–141 Queen Street East. The Four Happy Restaurant today occupies one section of the ground floor.

After buying the overalls, the visitor bought what would turn out to be his murder weapon — the razor-sharp knife that he would use four days later to kill Jessie. The *St. Marys Argus* of October 22, 1894, detailed the purchase: "A clerk in Mr. J.C. Gilpin's hardware store sold a stranger … an IXL pocket knife, for which was paid 28 cents."

In 1894 Gilpin's store was located in the Guest Block, the limestone building at the southeast corner of Queen and Wellington Streets, opposite the former A.H. Lofft building. The Guest Block houses three storefronts. Records from 1895 show that the Eedy publishing company occupied the easternmost offices, and a bank took up the westernmost unit. By deduction, J.C. Gilpin must have rented the store in the middle. Today it is numbered 140 Queen Street East and serves as the administrative offices for the Canadian Baseball Hall of Fame and Museum.

ST. MARYS JUNCTION STATION

Although it now stands derelict, the original train station at the northeast end of St. Marys remains protected by a fence and a national historic site designation. Solidly built of locally quarried limestone by the Grand Trunk Railway in 1858, it served for more than eighty years as a junction between the company's Toronto–Sarnia line and a branch running to London. Architectural distinctions include circular window vents, decorative chimneys, and a series of French doors along the front and back.

Documentation is sketchy, but American inventor Thomas Edison, known especially for creating the phonograph and incandescent light bulb, is said to have worked a few night shifts at the station. For several months as a sixteen-year-old in 1863 and 1864, he worked for the Grand Trunk Railway as a telegraph operator based in Stratford. In October 1894, Amédée Chattelle would have walked by the station on his way to Stratford and Listowel.

A weathered sign still hangs from the roof of the derelict St. Marys Junction train station, built of local limestone in 1858 and now a national historic site. The tramp would have passed it on the tracks on his way to Stratford.

CHAPTER 25

Fryfogel's Tavern: Perth County's First Settler

AMÉDÉE CHATTELLE CLAIMED he did not head north to Listowel. "To hell with Listowel," he told his interrogators on his first morning at Stratford Jail. Instead, he followed the railway east from Stratford to Shakespeare and New Hamburg, he said, then hopped a freight train to Guelph. He was lying, but anybody tracing Chattelle's route today would do well to detour east anyway to visit one of Perth County's heritage jewels, Fryfogel's Tavern.

Sebastian Fryfogel, in a photograph taken late in life, comes across as a cultured man. His dress is formal, his bearing erect, his face intelligent, and his head crowned with flowing white hair, accenting his bushy beard. He was born in 1791, the son of a Swiss innkeeper, near Basel. When he was seven, the family moved to Pennsylvania in the United States. He later married Mary Eby and in 1827 travelled north with her and their five children to a British wilderness outpost in what is now Waterloo County.

His timing was perfect. That same year, a settler-immigrant company, the Canada Company, established an office at what is now Guelph. The firm had acquired the Huron Tract, a British land charter of more than

Pioneering innkeeper Sebastian Fryfogel comes across as a cultured man in an undated portrait. He and his wife, Mary, are recognized as Perth County's first white settlers.

one million acres (more than four hundred thousand hectares). From a point just outside present-day New Hamburg, the tract widened west-ward into a triangle extending to the Lake Huron coast. Crews began constructing a stagecoach route from Guelph to the lake at Goderich. Over swampy sections, they placed logs tightly together to form what was called a "corduroy road," ribbed like corduroy and just as bumpy. Coaches could cover only thirty-two kilometres a day. At intervals along the way, inns were to be built, and Canada Company officer Anthony Van Egmond recruited Fryfogel to build the first one just east of what is now the village of Shakespeare. The agreement came with a plot of land, an annuity, and the distinction of becoming the first white settler in Perth County.

As road crews pushed through the thick Canadian forest, Fryfogel erected a preliminary stagecoach inn built of logs. Few details survive of those early days, but in 1834 a Scottish immigrant named George Elmslie mentioned the tavern twice in his rudimentary diary. "He was the original busy Canadian settler," Elmslie wrote of Fryfogel. "When we called, he was making a belt to put a small bell around the neck of a young ... doe [that was running among the children]."

The diarist continued in his basic style: "We had some remnants of dinner only consisting of potatoes, soup which being hungry and nothing else to get got we ate up.... The evening was fine ... [Mary Fryfogel] returned and some provisions had been procured, still we drank our tea without sugar ... whiskey helped."

Elmslie proceeded to Stratford, then returned to Fryfogel's Tavern, or Inn (the terms were synonymous at the time). "We found an Indian skinning two deer he had shot," he wrote. "Fryfogel bought the [hindquarters] of both.... At tea, we had excellent deer steak but a little over down [sic]."

Backwoods life might have been primitive, but Fryfogel proved a resourceful entrepreneur. He and Mary continued having children, twelve altogether, and in 1844 — seventeen years after arriving — he constructed the Georgian neoclassical brick-and-stone building that survives today as the last of the Huron Road stagecoach inns.

In 1856 the railway came through. The tracks still run two hundred metres behind the building, the same ones Chattelle falsely said he took. With the train traffic, Stratford grew as the main assembly point for settlers entering the district, and both stagecoach travel and Fryfogel's business correspondingly declined. The family, however, stayed on. Sebastian continued as a prominent local figure, serving in a number of public positions, including as district councillor, militia captain, magistrate, and the first Perth County warden. Mary died on the estate in 1871 at the age of seventy-two. Sebastian died two years later at eighty-one.

After their deaths, the inn stayed in the family, functioning variously as a residence, a cheese factory, and a restaurant. In the 1960s, descendants bequeathed it to the volunteer Stratford Perth Heritage Foundation, which seeks to restore the building and reopen it to the public, perhaps as a restaurant and bed and breakfast. Although the relaunch still looks far off, major structural and electrical work has been completed, and the walls have been stripped of paint and wallpaper. The volunteers mount fundraising events in the former ballroom and dining room, and hold special open-house days.

To stir further interest, they also offer guided tours to the public during July and August. Ironically, the best time to go might be now rather than after completion. Rarely do restoration crews admit outsiders to a work-in-progress, a heritage home stripped and sanded to its bare plaster and raw floorboards.

"A lot of people don't want us to do anything more," says foundation member Rebekah Kielek. "Photographers love it. One woman is coming back to get her wedding photos shot here."

Photographers love how parts of some walls are stripped to the laths in the reconstruction phase of historic Fryfogel's Tavern. The Stratford Perth Heritage Foundation gives seasonal tours.

Kielek takes me through the building. We start inside the main front door, which because of the inn's symmetrical Georgian design means we are standing in a central hallway, with rooms to either side.

"The walls look kind of mouldy," she says, "but what you see is the original imitation-marble painting. In the wilderness, Sebastian had no way to get actual marble, but he wanted to make the inn look kind of grand. He hired an artist to stay here and paint the hallways in faux marble. This is one of the last surviving original examples in Canada."

High along the corridor wall run the remains of a rack for hanging the long cloaks worn by stagecoach riders. A door opens to the former tavern room, featuring original cabinets built into the wall. The room admitted men only. Women would use the parlour across the hall.

Kielek leads me through the parlour, the former dining room, and Fryfogel's former office. Downstairs, she shows me the pioneer kitchen with its giant open fireplace, still equipped with its original cooking crane. When restoration crews sanded the basement stairwell walls, they uncovered Fryfogel's signature, which can still be seen. Back on the ground floor, we ascend a set of worn, wooden stairs to the upper rooms.

"This is the original staircase," Kielek says, "nearly one hundred and seventy-five years of people walking up and down."

A small back bedroom once gave privacy to an individual or a family with money. A grand adjoining guest dormitory doubled as a ballroom for political events and community entertainment. Across the hall was the trunk room. "If you have twenty guests and they all bring a large trunk, where do you put them all?" Kielek asks rhetorically.

Parts of the walls are stripped to the laths, thin strips of wood nailed closely together to support plaster. "The restoration workers have exposed the laths on purpose to show how uneven they were, not like [later] Edwardian houses," Kielek says. "One of the challenges is trying to imitate these techniques to make them historically accurate."

Next comes the biggest surprise of the tour. In a spacious front bedroom, over the fireplace, a large fresco from the mantelpiece to the ceiling depicts the splendour of Niagara Falls, a natural wonder of the world. Restoration workers uncovered it beneath multiple layers of paint

In the front bedroom, under layers of paint and wallpaper, restoration workers were surprised to discover a large fresco of Niagara Falls. "To see this major Canadian landmark depicted here would have been a delight," says heritage foundation member Rebekah Kielek.

and wallpaper. "To see this major Canadian landmark depicted here would have been a delight," Kielek says. "Most settlers would never have been able to actually visit the falls. By stagecoach it would have been too far away."

The mural is framed in faux bird's-eye maple. Traces of paint suggest the baseboards were enhanced in the same way, and part of one wall is painted to look like wood panelling. In the ballroom, crews uncovered a second fresco, but it is a more generic landscape than the first. It is also badly damaged. When wallpaper still covered it, somebody drove a stovepipe through its centre.

Damaged or not, the second fresco further adds to evidence of a once beautifully decorated building. Fryfogel might have been roughing it in the wilderness, but from his Swiss boyhood he retained a sense of cultured living.

FRYFOGEL TOMBSTONES

To the right of the parking lot entrance, near the road, three nineteenth-century headstones stand flush against one another. They were gathered in the 1920s from a cemetery plot in a nearby field. The stones memorialize Sebastian Fryfogel; his father, Jacob, killed by a falling tree branch in 1836 after moving in with the family; and Sebastian and Mary's six-year-old son, Henry, accidentally poisoned in 1842.

THE ARBORETUM

Just as the heritage foundation is restoring the inn, so the group is restoring the wilderness around it. Since 2010, on the inn's two hectares of land, volunteers have been replanting the native trees, flowers, and bushes that the original settlers worked so hard to clear. "This project is of great importance due to the ongoing loss of original forest cover in the Perth County area," says Reg White, who helped initiate the project. "Many species are rare or are disappearing entirely." Participation from the University of Guelph, the Grand River Conservation Authority, and the Niagara Horticultural School has helped bring attention to the arboretum as a monarch-butterfly way station. It is publicly accessible year-round.

CHAPTER 26
Baden: The Flax Kings

CASTLE KILBRIDE TO SOME PEOPLE looks stuck in the middle of nowhere, surrounded by farmers' fields. The national historic site and museum serves as a reminder, however, that in nineteenth-century Ontario almost every town and village was engaged in industrial activity. They milled grain, planed lumber, built farm machinery, constructed carriages, and manufactured pianos. The village of Baden, midway between Kitchener and Stratford, was no different. Early settlers established a flour mill. They later built a second flour mill, two sawmills, an iron foundry, and ultimately the J. & J. Livingston Linseed Oil Company, the largest flax-producing enterprise in North America.

Many people today know flaxseed, or linseed, as a health food. They value its dietary fibre, plant-based protein, and anti-inflammatory omega-3 fatty acids. In the nineteenth century, however, the entire flax plant went to make important industrial commodities. From the stem came thread to make linen, canvas, twine, and high-quality paper. From the seed came oil used in linoleum, printing inks, wood finishers, and high-quality paints. Most producers operated at a local level. J. & J. Livingston's innovation was to produce flax on an industrial scale and

Husband-and-wife folk duo Mike and Diana Erb, who perform as Twas Now, play a summer concert at the foot of Castle Kilbride, James Livingston's charming 1877 Baden home, now a national historic site. James and his elder brother John, of Listowel, reigned as North America's flax kings.

to involve itself in every stage of the process, from farming to manufacturing to distributing.

"J. & J." stood for brothers John and James, "the flax kings." They lived a rags-to-riches story. They grew up as sons of a cotton weaver in East Kilbride, Scotland, near Glasgow, and in 1854 crossed the ocean together. John was twenty, James sixteen. In New York State and Canada West, as Ontario was called, they took labouring jobs on flax farms, rose to management positions, and in 1864 — ten years after leaving home — founded their own company. They began by buying land and growing flax near Wellesley, in Waterloo County. Within three years they moved their main operations to Baden.

After building a flax mill in Baden, the largest in Canada, the brothers expanded to other southwestern Ontario villages, including Blyth, Palmerston, Linwood, Brussels, and Listowel. They branched into Manitoba and Michigan. Both brothers prospered as smart, hard-working businessmen, but younger brother James proved the greater entrepreneur and visionary. He stayed in Baden to run the headquarters. Elder brother John moved to manage the Listowel-area operations.

As their fortunes grew the Livingstons planned their mansions. James went first. Baden at the time was a village of mainly German Lutheran immigrants who practised modesty over ostentation. James integrated by marrying Louisa Liersch, a woman of German origin, in 1861, and by raising their twelve children — eight girls and four boys — in English and German. In 1877, however, he decided to exercise his independent taste in a new home. At a time when almost the whole village extended south of the main township road, he chose the north side. On a knoll slightly back from the road, at the end of a heart-shape drive, he built an exquisite two-storey, yellow-brick mansion of Italianate design. It had large bay windows and a columned porch, and was crowned by an open-sided lookout gallery, or belvedere. He called the estate Castle Kilbride, after the Livingston family birthplace in Scotland.

If the home's exterior was striking, the interior was even more so. In 1878, James hired German-born artist Henry Schasstein, then living in Preston, now part of Cambridge, to decorate the principal downstairs rooms with linseed-oil-based paint. "James Livingston … paid homage to the product that made him rich," architectural historian Jacqueline Hucker says in her paper, "Decorative Mural Painting of Castle Kilbride."

"The paintings," says Parks Canada, partly to explain the home's national historic site designation, "are outstanding examples of late 19th-century, domestic, painted mural decoration. [They are valued for] their high level of execution, their fine decorative quality, their cohesive integration with the architecture of the house, and their generally good condition."

In Renaissance Revival style, Schasstein painted elaborate wall and ceiling murals populated by cherubs, musicians, warriors, and gods. He worked from a vibrant palette. In the library alone he used thirty-eight colours. He also displayed a special talent for a technique called *trompe l'oeil*, meaning "trick the eye," a difficult skill aimed at conjuring up three dimensions on flat surfaces. In the central hallway, he painted illusory columns and floral bouquets, and in the library created the impression of tassels hanging from the ceiling along the walls.

In other details of the home, as well, James displayed a refined artistic taste. He hired skilled woodcarvers to trim the doors and windows. He imported fireplaces of Carrara marble, the same sugar-white stone from which Jessie's statue was carved. His bedroom ceiling he finished with a single piece of fine linen, and he became an early patron and friend of Homer Watson, one of Canada's most accomplished landscape artists and an influence on the later Group of Seven. Watson lived in nearby Doon. "We're especially fond of the Homer Watson painting *Old Mill and Stream*," Castle Kilbride director and curator Tracy Loch says. "It's from 1879, a very significant work."

The painting is considered the sister of *The Pioneer Mill*, which Canada's governor general, the Marquis of Lorne, bought in 1880 as a gift for Queen Victoria. The marquis was married to Princess Louise, the sixth of the monarch's nine children. His gift, which still hangs in the private quarters of Windsor Castle, brought Watson international renown.

Also in 1880, three years after James built Castle Kilbride, elder brother John in Listowel built Livingston Manor. It has a more massive appearance than the Baden home and features a type of widow's walk instead of a belvedere, but in many ways the house is a copycat. Both were designed by the same architect, David Gingerich, and both are built of yellow brick in the Italianate style, with an identical central-hall plan, the same ornate wooden staircase, and similar front bay windows.

Livingston Manor also pays homage to linseed oil. To decorate the interior, John hired Hungarian-born artist Karl Muller, who lived with the couple and their six children for two years while executing the work. If not quite of Schasstein's calibre, Muller was a fine artist. He likewise employed the *trompe l'oeil* technique, and in exuberant murals depicted cherub-like children at play in various seasons of the year. Like his younger brother, John also commissioned detailed woodwork, handcrafted brass door handles, and beautifully carved, marble fireplaces.

Neither John nor James kept a diary, and little evidence remains of their intimate thoughts or feelings. One extraordinary detail about their relationship, however, surfaced after John's death. The brothers shared a single bank account.

"It was a remarkable example of mutual confidence and affection," court judge Lord Sumner wrote of the forty-year partnership. "The brothers came to Canada as quite young men and agreed that from their earnings they would have a common purse and in all enterprises a common venture. This plan was so whole-heartedly carried out that they built their houses and bought their furniture with funds taken by each at will from the common stock. They drew [from] it as required for household expenses, and never to the last day of John Livingston's life did they strike a balance or arrange a division between themselves."

James and Louisa had twelve children. John and his wife, Anna, had six. On that basis, the common account might seem to favour younger brother James. On the other hand, James was the driving force of the flax empire and shared everything with John, an arrangement that clearly favoured the elder brother. Maybe the younger brother felt a debt to the elder one from the time they left Scotland at such a young age. Maybe the brothers simply enjoyed a special fraternal bond. Even their corporate name gave them equal billing as "J. & J. Livingston," rather than "John & James Livingston," or "James & John Livingston." When the partnership ended with John's death, however, the courts rejected claims to half the fortune by John's heirs, awarding a more modest settlement. "The leading spirit in everything was James," wrote Lord Sumner, an appeals court judge in London, England. "He was the younger, the abler, and the better educated of the two. John managed the firm's mill at Listowel, where he lived, and there his active part of the business ended."

John's death came suddenly. On May 21, 1896, the elder brother awoke at his usual early hour and went for a walk. He got as far as the downtown Bank of Hamilton and on his return stopped at the Imperial Hotel, across from his house on Main Street West. "He sat for a few minutes chatting with [hotel owner] Mr. Kraus, when he suddenly put his hand to his chest complaining of a severe pain," one local newspaper reported. "He was asked to lie down, Mr. Kraus volunteering to get a mustard plaster to put on, but Mr. Livingston said he would go home and immediately crossed the street to his own residence, where he was at once assisted to bed and medical assistance called. He grew rapidly worse and in less than twenty minutes from the time he felt the trouble coming on, he had expired."

John was sixty-two. His burial took place in Fairview Cemetery three days after his collapse, on a Sunday, the same day Jessie Keith's statue was to be unveiled. That morning, a special train left Baden carrying James and Louisa, other family members, more than a hundred company employees, and members of the Masonic Order, of which James was a prominent member and to which John had also belonged. At Stratford another hundred people boarded. "All six coaches were crowded," the *Listowel Banner* said. "A special train also left Kincardine on Sunday morning and brought in a large delegation from points along that line. Large numbers also drove from the neighbouring towns, and ... made up such a concourse of people as has seldom been gathered together at any one time in the town."

In a separate story, the *Banner* told of the coincidental Jessie Keith statue dedication. For different reasons, both deaths touched almost everybody in the district, and by early afternoon an estimated three thousand people were gathered in the graveyard. How many came for the Livingston funeral and how many for the Keith ceremony is not recorded, but the graves were close to each other and most visitors attended both.

After his brother's death, James continued to excel in business and in other ways. He renamed the firm the Dominion Linseed Oil Company and established a mill and office in Montreal. He expanded into other areas of manufacturing and into banking and insurance. By then he was also a politician. After making Baden prosperous and employing hundreds of workers, he proved an easy choice for village reeve, then as the riding's member of the Ontario Legislature. In 1882, he ran successfully for Parliament and served two terms in Prime Minister Wilfrid Laurier's Liberal government, rising to minister of mines and northern affairs.

Livingston Manor and Castle Kilbride stand as lasting testaments to the flax kings. The Listowel home stayed in the Livingston family until 1951 and functions now as an upscale retirement home, misspelled as Livingstone Manor, with an *e*. Castle Kilbride at one point seemed doomed. It remained in the family until 1988, when granddaughter Laura Louise sold the property to a developer. An auction was held and all the contents sold. After the developer's plans failed, however, and after the property sat empty for five years, the township found a way to purchase the estate.

The hero of the rescue effort was Jim Miller, a local antiques dealer and auctioneer. At the Castle Kilbride auction, he went into debt to buy key treasures and kept careful records of every item sold. With the announcement that the house was to be saved, he worked with the township to reacquire as many of the original Livingston furnishings as possible. Pieces keep coming in.

"A lot of people who were here for the 1988 auction are now downsizing," museum director Loch says. "Their kids are not into antiques and they call us."

More than 70 percent of the auctioned material has since been returned, including one of the museum's most-prized objects, Homer Watson's painting, *Old Mill and Stream*. It hangs once more in its original spot over the piano in the parlour.

THE BADEN HOTEL

The building is better known today as E.J.'s Tavern, no longer letting rooms but still attracting customers. In 1874, three years before James Livingston began Castle Kilbride, hotelier Christoph Kraus built the red-brick landmark across the street.

Tin tiles from the hotel's early days still decorate the ceiling above the bar. Each is ornamentally stamped around the outside, like a picture frame. Within each frame is painted a floral arrangement or summer landscape. One work depicts a millpond at twilight, another a farmhouse with buggy tracks to the door. Several portray waterfalls. Over the years, people started wondering who might have created the artwork, and a legend developed about an itinerant nineteenth-century painter working to pay his room and board.

In 2005, the Kitchener-Waterloo Art Gallery embarked on what it called "The Baden Hotel Project." The gallery commissioned an illustrated booklet celebrating the tiles. To write the text, the editor hired Stratford novelist Jane Urquhart, who was then starting work on her sixth novel, *A Map of Glass*. By coincidence, one of her main characters was to be an itinerant

Stamped tin tiles painted with landscapes and floral patterns decorate the ceiling above the bar of the 1874 Baden Hotel, popularly known today as E.J.'s Tavern. In her novel *A Map of Glass*, Stratford writer Jane Urquhart conjures up the unknown artist who created the pictures.

nineteenth-century artist named Branwell Woodman. Her text for the gallery helped shape the novel's storyline. "Branwell, I decided, would come to Baden," Urquhart says in the gallery booklet about her fictional narrative. "The weather would be bad, and he would be forced to put up at the tavern."

In the novel, Branwell paints both the tin ceiling tiles at the Baden Hotel and the upstairs bedroom murals at Fryfogel's Tavern, thirteen kilometres to the west. In reality, two different artists are thought to have executed the works, with the Fryfogel paintings considered the more ambitious.

A later researcher discovered that the Baden tiles were not painted in the nineteenth century after all, and not for room and board. They were completed sometime after 1920 by a man hired specifically for the job. The information comes from an unpublished memoir by Edna Stiefelmeyer, wife of John Stiefelmeyer, owner of the Baden Hotel from 1920 to 1946. John met a painter working at Kitchener's Walper Hotel, which had been built in 1893 and still operates today. "[John] invited this man to come to Baden some time if he was out of work," Edna writes, without naming the man or specifying when he took up the offer.

The hired illustrator painted twenty-seven tiles, Edna said. One was later damaged beyond repair. Two others had to come down and now hang separately on the wall beside the bar. The other twenty-four remain in place, unique historic works by a still-unknown hand.

PUDDICOMBE HOUSE

Visitors cannot stay overnight at Castle Kilbride, but they can sleep at the former mansion of James Livingston's political rival in nearby New Hamburg. The house is open as an eight-room hotel and restaurant. Swiss immigrant Samuel Merner built the place in 1868, also in the elegant Italianate style, with four-metre ceilings, ornamental bay windows, and an outsized porch. Livingston's creation nine years later might partly have been an act of competition.

Merner began his career as a farmer. He soon established a blacksmith shop in New Hamburg, expanded into wagons and carriages, and later branched into flour-milling, newspaper publishing, and fire insurance, among other interests. Throughout the 1870s and 1880s, he reigned as the village's dominant personality and entrepreneur, just as Livingston did in Baden. In 1878, Merner ran successfully for Parliament, serving one term in the Conservative government of Prime Minister John A. Macdonald. Four years later, Livingston unseated him as the Liberal challenger. Merner was appointed to the Senate.

In 1888, twenty years after building the home, Merner sold it to another successful former farmer, Robert Puddicombe, in whose family it remained for eight decades. In 1968, the property changed hands, and in 2004 Lyle and Karen Cressman bought and painstakingly restored it. Family members still run the hotel and a new event centre on the same property.

THE PRIME MINISTERS PATH

A bronze sculpture of Sir John A. Macdonald, Canada's first prime minister, stands behind two empty chairs near the main entrance to Castle Kilbride. Symbolically, he invites the English- and French-speaking populations of British North America to unite as the Dominion of Canada and, more literally, invites visitors to sit for a picture.

Instead of standing on the plinth, Canada's fourteenth prime minister, Lester B. Pearson, is depicted sitting beside it with his shoes off. Sculptor Ruth Abernethy cast the disarming work in bronze.

The artwork marks the start of the Prime Ministers Path, which is eventually to include representations of every Canadian prime minister since Confederation. In 2018, the fifth figure was unveiled, a likeness of Kim Campbell, who served for four months in 1993.

"If you were prime minister you are included, no matter what anybody says about your significance," says former Kitchener-Waterloo Collegiate principal Jim Rodger, co-founder of the project with Dave Caputo, chair of the Sandvine telecommunications company in Waterloo. "You were a leader of this country, you had influence."

The first sculptor hired was Ruth Abernethy, from nearby Wellesley, to create the Sir John A. piece. She has since contributed a disarming work depicting Canada's fourteenth prime minister, Lester B. Pearson, sitting on a plinth with his shoes off. Abernethy is also known for her 1997 *Raising the Tent* sculpture outside the Festival Theatre in Stratford. The first five works at Castle Kilbride depict Macdonald, King, Pearson, Campbell, and Canada's eighth prime minister, Sir Robert Borden.

Originally, the sculpture collection was to grace Victoria Park in downtown Kitchener, until activists objected to celebrating what they called "corrupt white men." Subsequently, the works were to adorn the grounds of Wilfrid Laurier University, until protesters similarly accused authorities of perpetuating "a white hetero-male historical narrative of power."

Castle Kilbride made a natural alternative. James Livingston served two terms as a Member of Parliament in Prime Minister Wilfrid Laurier's Liberal government, part of that time as minister of mines and northern affairs. His rival in New Hamburg, Samuel Merner, served as an MP for the same riding for the Conservatives. More important, perhaps, the people running the museum were prepared to publicly assert respect for Canada's heritage.

CHAPTER 27
Stratford: The Prisoner's Dock

THE IDEA WAS TO strip the pine tar from all the wood surfaces. Thick, black tar — once widely used as a wood preservative — covered the doors, baseboards, window frames, staircases, and all the original wood furniture at the Perth County Court House. Brian Priestap took charge of removing it. With a small crew, he started in the fall of 1981 and by mid-1983 he and his team were working in the main, upstairs courtroom, two storeys high, where Amédée Chattelle had stood trial nearly one hundred years earlier.

One night, the workers were stripping the prisoner's dock, the same dock Chattelle had occupied. Half an hour before midnight Priestap called a halt to the work. It was time to clean up. The crew had to make everything tidy again for court the next morning, which meant putting the dock back in place. For stripping, it had sat detached from the court railings in a steel pan, which was collecting lacquer thinner dripping off the wood.

"I said, 'Okay, that's enough, let's get cleaned up,'" Priestap recalls of the moment. "That's when a young lad struck a match — we could smoke anywhere in the building in those days. As he was walking by the prisoner's dock, he lit a stick match and kaboom. The whole thing went up."

Occupying prime real estate at the head of Ontario Street, the Perth County Court House stands as one of Stratford's best loved heritage buildings. In the main upstairs courtroom, graced by tall windows to the right of the tower, Amédée Chattelle went on trial for the murder of Jessie Keith.

Lacquer thinner is more volatile than gasoline. Maybe the match broke into the pan, or maybe flaming sulphur sprayed into the pan, or maybe nothing from the match reached the pan at all. A mere spark could have ignited the fumes. One man still washing the dock was blown backward, his hair singed.

"Grab the extinguishers! Call the fire department!" Priestap shouted.

As the flames shot upward, he pulled down a set of enormous blue drapes at the back of the room and threw them on the flames. Then he pulled down a second set, destroying the curtains but saving the building.

"We had it just about out when the firemen got here," Priestap recalls. "It was just smoking a little and they hit it with a little bit of water. Whoosh — it was over."

The courthouse survives as one of the jewels of Stratford's architectural heritage. It also occupies one of the city's choicest lots, looming at the head of Ontario Street on land where Stratford's first mayor, John Daly, built his home. Anybody entering the city from the east can see the courthouse in the distance.

A hand raised in a sign of benediction, or blessing, features in a terracotta embellishment above the St. Andrew Street entrance to the Perth County Court House. Symbolism in the courthouse is everywhere.

It opened in 1887, the year of Queen Victoria's Golden Jubilee, her fiftieth year on the throne. Years of tolerating the bad smells and dilapidation of the original courthouse across the river came to an end. "The transition from the old to the new room is from the extreme of dinginess and discomfort to a chamber fit for a monarch," the *Stratford Beacon* said when it opened.

A tourist pamphlet about the building calls it "an excellent example of High Victorian architecture." Highlights include the off-centre medieval tower, and the bold colour combination of yellow brick, pink Credit Valley sandstone, terracotta decorative touches, and brownish-mauve paint over the wood trim.

The building still functions as a courthouse, which means it is open to the public. Anybody can walk in and look around. Inside the front entrance, a marble tablet bears the names of officials and crafts people involved in construction, including architect George Durand. Colourful mosaic tiles cover the floors. The main staircase, directly opposite the entrance, features a pillar of carved oak, the flowers representing the four parts of the British Isles — thistle for Scotland, rose for England, shamrock for Ireland, and leek for Wales. Symbolism is everywhere. Large stained-glass windows over the main landing depict, in part, coats of arms for all seven Canadian provinces of the time. The Perth County coat of arms also appears, with a sheaf of wheat for the main cash crop, a train for industrial progress, two ploughs for agriculture, and a beehive signifying human industriousness.

The main courtroom has changed little since Chattelle's time. The tall, arched windows are the same. The judge's and clerk's ornamental benches, also designed by architect Durand, are original to the room, and the public gallery, seating two hundred people, features the same pine pews on which William, Jane, and Ida Keith sat for Chattelle's trial.

After the fire destroyed the prisoner's box in 1983, Priestap looked for a way to duplicate it. He had spent most of his career in antique trading and restoration, and knew almost everybody in the business. He took the charred remains to Chuck Wilhelm, a master lather, refinisher, and co-owner of Stratford's Brodgar GuildWorks.

"Could you possibly replace this?" Priestap asked.

"I'll have a look," Wilhelm said, and produced a replica almost indistinguishable from the original.

The main artifact missing from the room as it looked in 1894 is the chandelier. Chattelle would have sat directly under a magnificent two-tiered fixture lit by coal gas, but somebody stole it, Priestap says. James Anderson, Perth County's first archivist, apparently knew where it went. "He always said it is in two pieces and hangs in two separate Stratford homes," Priestap says. "He would always say, 'You and I are going to get that chandelier before I die. We're going to get it and put it back up.'"

Anderson served from 1972 to 1991 as archivist and as one of the county's foremost heritage champions. He died in 1994, however, without ever revealing the addresses of the two suspect houses. His secret died with him. Maybe one day, out of feelings of civic duty, the chandelier keepers will come forward, Priestap says. The original 1887 ornament under which Chattelle stood might yet again light the courtroom.

STRATFORD JAIL

Architect George Durand designed a neighbouring jail to match the court building and disguised it to look outwardly like a house. Chief jailer Hugh Nichol resided in the building with his family from 1886, when the jail opened, until his death in 1921. The building still functions as a jail, which means that although visitors can see where Chattelle stood trial, no access is given to his old cell in the upper west corridor or to the courtyard where he was hanged.

One of Stratford's most visible citizens, chief jailer Hugh Nichol enjoyed wearing a ceremonial kilt. When the new jail opened in 1886, he moved in with his family and died there, still on the job, at seventy-nine in 1921.

CHAPTER 28

Stratford: The Coroner's Saddest Inquest

DR. JAMES RANKIN, the coroner at the time of Jessie Keith's death, is remembered as one of Stratford's most prominent early medical and political figures. "One of the recognized leaders of the medical profession in this city," the *Stratford Daily Herald* once said of him. In 1908 and again in 1921, he also won election as a Liberal Member of Parliament under prime ministers Wilfrid Laurier and Mackenzie King, respectively. A few years later, he was appointed to the Senate.

A family studio photo from the mid-1890s shows him as a balding, avuncular-looking man with a walrus moustache and a cheerful countenance. With him are his wife, Mary Jane, looking strong and no-nonsense, his teenage daughters, Jessie and Ethelwyn, and his son, Ramsay, shown at the age of eight or nine. They lived at 256 Erie Street, in a handsome two-storey yellow-brick house with high ceilings that still stands today, two blocks from the former office on the Market Square that Rankin once shared with a Dr. Cannon.

As a coroner, Rankin must have witnessed many tough moments. One would have been the night he walked into the swampy wood and pulled back the sheet to view the crimson-soaked petticoat around Jessie Keith's throat. His most difficult time, however, must have come at a coroner's

Dr. James Rankin, coroner, sits for an undated portrait with his wife Mary Jane, his daughters Jessie, left, and Ethelwyn, and his son, Ramsay, born in 1888. The boy became a university hockey star and medical doctor but met an untimely end.

inquest that he attended twenty-three years later as an observer. His only son, Ramsay, by then also a medical doctor, had been found dead at a friend's apartment in Montreal. The first newspaper reports suggested murder.

"It appears that a party took place at an apartment at 424 St. Catherine [S]treet [W]est," The Canadian Press said of the incident of Tuesday, May 31, 1921. "Around 11 o'clock, occupants in other apartments heard the front door bell ring. The door was opened and almost immediately a quarrel ensued.

"A sound of crashing glass was heard," the report continued, "and when an investigation was made Dr. [Ramsay] Rankin was found lying on the stairs in a pool of his own blood. He was in his underclothes. It is thought that Dr. Rankin was first stabbed with a knife and then thrown through a door, the glass in which cut him in several places…. [O]n the floor was found a large bread knife."

Ramsay was thirty-two years old and married with two children. By all outward appearances, he also seemed poised to take his place in Stratford's established professional circles. His life had seen a string of successes. After finishing high school in Stratford, he attended the University of Toronto for two years and, in 1911, transferred to McGill University to complete his medical studies. There he shone in every possible way — academically, socially, and athletically. "During his student days at McGill he was probably the most prominent and popular undergraduate in the whole institution," The Canadian Press said at the time of his death. "An athlete of outstanding prowess he was largely responsible [as captain] for the great victories gained by the senior McGill hockey team."

In 1914, at the outset of the First World War, Ramsay enlisted as an army medical officer and served overseas. Afterward, he founded a medical practice in Saskatchewan, then relocated back to Stratford. Two days before his death, he arrived in Montreal to conduct a business transaction and visit old friends.

He died on a Tuesday night. On Thursday morning, a coroner's inquest convened to determine whether a crime had been committed, the room packed mostly with Ramsay's friends from his McGill days. James Rankin, the father, had arrived by train with Stratford mayor Walter Gregory, a cousin.

Four people detained by police on the night in question were also present, two men and two women. One of the men was W.R. McEachren of the Iron Mountain Metal and Land Company, a brother-in-law of Ramsay's wife. The other was J.P. Brown, tenant of the apartment where the death occurred. The two women were identified as Miss M. Amyot and Miss C. Amyot, apparently sisters and occupants of the apartment next door.

A pathologist testified that Ramsay Rankin died of hemorrhaging from four major lacerations. Like Jessie Keith, he had bled to death. Broken glass almost certainly caused two of the gashes, the pathologist said, one shard having lodged in the abdomen. Whether a sharp instrument, such as the bread knife, caused the other two wounds could not be determined, he said.

Slowly the truth emerged. On Tuesday afternoon, Ramsay and Brown, the tenant, started drinking copiously together. They drank a bottle of whisky at Brown's apartment, then went to a hotel to drink beer. How much beer they drank Brown was unable to say. He hadn't kept track. When the friends arrived back at the apartment, they started drinking gin.

At 9:30 in the evening, by prior arrangement, McEachren arrived. He had drawn up a partnership deal between Brown and Ramsay concerning oil leases in northern Alberta. Once the papers were signed, McEachren phoned a taxi to return to a restaurant where he had been dining with friends.

The ring of the front doorbell mentioned in the initial press report might have been the cab driver. The drinking party might have been loud, but no quarrel took place, the witnesses said.

Brown went to the kitchen to mix gin cocktails and heard a crash. Rushing back into the main room, he saw Ramsay sprawled in the hallway, apparently having fallen through a glass panel in the door. He might have been using the knife to slice lemons for the drinks. The women next door heard the breaking glass but did not leave their apartment. Brown called an ambulance. A few hours later Ramsay died at Western Hospital.

"Death by accident," the coroner ruled, and Dr. Rankin and Mayor Gregory returned to Stratford with the body.

CHAPTER 29
Stratford: Death by Fire

POLICE CHIEF JOHN MCCARTHY narrowly escaped death when he fell under the moving train at Listowel station trying to get Amédée Chattelle aboard. Nineteen years later, while fighting a fire in Stratford, he never stood a chance.

The McCarthys were among Stratford's earliest settlers. In 1832, John Augustus McCarthy Sr. broke a wagon wheel near a camp on the present site of the Lion's Pool. The camp belonged to the Canada Company, the chartered land agency responsible for opening a large swath of Upper Canada to new settlement. McCarthy, so the story goes, stopped for repairs and stayed. He later became Stratford's first police officer. His eldest son, Thomas, Stratford's first white baby, also became a police constable, and a younger son, John Jr., rose to the post of "chief constable," or chief of police.

On May 13, 1913, shortly after midnight, lightning struck the tall, elegant steeple of downtown Knox Presbyterian Church, at Waterloo and Ontario Streets. The tip of the spire ignited and the structure burst into flames. Firefighters arrived in a horse-drawn wagon carrying a steam-powered water pump, but jets from the hoses couldn't reach the

Knox Church, Stratford, Ont., Canada

A vintage postcard shows the magnificent steeple of Knox Presbyterian Church before the night of May 13, 1913, when it drew a lightning strike and caught fire. A timber falling from the belfry onto the far side of the building killed the police chief, the fire chief, and a police constable.

blaze. The men climbed ladders up the building but the water still couldn't reach. By then a wind had come up, casting cinders across the roof and lighting small additional fires.

On the street below a crowd gathered. People stood in their night-clothes, and faces appeared in the windows of the Queen's Inn, kitty-corner from the church. About one in the morning, spectators watched the fiery skeleton of the steeple fall onto the church roof and break through in a number of places. The belfry supporting the steeple roared like a furnace. The firefighters were losing the battle.

At about one thirty, fire chief Hugh Durkin walked over to the west wall to adjust a ladder. Police chief McCarthy and constable Matthew Hamilton rushed to help, and as they repositioned the ladder part of the belfry collapsed. A burning timber two and a half metres long hit them both, killing them instantly. The beam missed Durkin, but a shower of bricks and wood buried him.

"As willing hands pulled [the debris] from him his last and only words were, 'Hurry, boys, hurry!'" the *Stratford Beacon* reported. "He then lapsed into unconsciousness."

Durkin died on the way to hospital. He was thirty-nine years old. McCarthy was sixty-six, Hamilton forty-six. The church was destroyed, although a Sunday school annex survived.

Two days later the city buried its dead. In the face of the terrible loss, Stratford did its best to show itself as intact and functioning. The morning began with the three bodies lying in open caskets at the men's respective homes. Three separate church services were held — Catholic for Durkin, Presbyterian for Hamilton, and Anglican for McCarthy.

At one in the afternoon, all Stratford shops and businesses closed for the day. Most factories also stopped work, and although the Grand Trunk Railway shops remained open, the factory whistle was silenced, and leave was granted to any worker wishing to attend the procession to the cemetery.

By two o'clock the three caskets lay in a row at the City Hall auditorium. Black fabric draped the front of the building and the indoor auditorium walls. The room was "packed to the doors," the *Stratford Beacon* said.

W.E. Millson, chairman of the Ministerial Association, led an ecumenical service that began with the hymn "My Faith Looks Up to Thee," sung by a fifty-member male choir put together from several churches and directed by Knox Presbyterian organist E.E. Pridham.

Shortly after three o'clock the procession to Avondale Cemetery began. In a city of 13,000 people, an estimated 16,000 lined the streets to watch. The Stratford Collegiate Institute Cadets fell into formation, rifles over left shoulders and drums solemnly muffled. The cadets had loosened the tension on their drumheads to deaden the resonance. Various other groups and fraternities coalesced behind them — city councillors, visiting municipal representatives, the Grand Trunk Railway Employees Band, the Oddfellows, the Knights of Columbus, visiting police and fire officials, Boer War and Fenian Raids veterans, the Catholic Mutual Benefit Association, the Ancient Order of Foresters, and the Woodmen of the World.

At equally spaced intervals, horse-drawn hearses conveyed the bodies of McCarthy, Durkin, and Hamilton, in that order. The cortège snaked along Downie Street, veered left onto Ontario Street, and continued around the Perth County Court House toward the graveyard.

"Men from every walk of life were present," the *Beacon* said, "their true realization of the enormity of the loss over-shadowing any petty differences there may have been between them. Many were the tears shed during the service and as the funeral cortege passed along the streets en route to the cemetery. No attempt was made, either to conceal the sorrow. It was pure, unaffected, wholehearted, and was but another reminder of the great gap which remains in the city's official ranks."

More than twenty years later, in 1936, elder brother Thomas McCarthy died at the age of ninety-four. The *Stratford Beacon Herald* recalled the Jessie Keith inquest at Listowel as one of the most intense assignments of his career, saying, "[he] faced a mob of angry citizens who wanted to lynch the murderer."

Similarly, police chief John McCarthy might have been commemorated for getting Chattelle safely back to Stratford, but is remembered now instead for his tragic death. In 1915, the Knox Presbyterian congregation rebuilt its church in a different style, without a spire. On May 13, 2013 —

On one of the saddest days in Stratford's history, a funeral procession carrying the bodies of police chief John McCarthy, fire chief Hugh Durkin, and constable Matthew Hamilton crawls along Ontario Street and turns in front of the Perth County Court House on May 15, 1913. All three died fighting a fire that destroyed Knox Presbyterian Church.

one hundred years after the inferno — civic leaders gathered to unveil a plaque to McCarthy, Durkin, and Hamilton in the church's east garden.

"The community remembers the sacrifice made by these brave and selfless heroes," the inscription says.

To coincide with the event, the Stratford Perth Museum mounted a special exhibition to honour the fallen men, its centrepiece a burnt piece of timber from the once elegant steeple.

CHAPTER 30
Stratford: The Rape and Murder of Mary Peake

FRANK ROUGHMOND SEEMED perfectly sane, his jailers said. "A model prisoner," they called him. "Well behaved and gave no trouble." He had been arrested in Listowel on vagrancy charges and sentenced to twenty days in Stratford Jail. When his term was up, the jailers returned his pipe, tobacco, jackknife, coloured handkerchiefs, and several packs of cards. At six o'clock in the morning on September 30, 1908, they released him, never thinking they would see him again that same afternoon.

"His actions in no way indicated insanity," the *Stratford Evening Beacon* paraphrased prison authorities as insisting afterward. "In fact he appeared to be sharp, quick witted and intelligent."

Roughmond was in the prime of his life. Thirty-four years old, six feet tall, and physically fit, he called himself a fortune-teller, or more specifically a palmist and phrenologist. He could read palms, he said, and tell a person's character and abilities from the size and shape of their skull. He was also a drinker and a tramp. He wore blue overalls, a blue jean jacket, a white straw hat, and eyeglasses with gold-coloured rims. Being from the Gaspé region of Quebec, he spoke heavily accented English and fluent French. He was also black.

On his release that morning, Roughmond made the rounds of the downtown Stratford hotels. At every stop he asked for a room and a drink, and at every stop he was eventually asked to leave. At the Albion Hotel, with twenty-three cents in his pocket, he ordered a drink and was served. He didn't appear drunk, patrons later said, but he wore out his welcome with his incessant talking. At the Commercial Hotel, he spoke incoherently, wandering from one subject to another. At the Queen's Hotel, apparently possessing twenty-five cents, he bought a drink of gin and a glass of lager. At the Cabinet Hotel, he persuaded a man to pay him twenty-five cents to tell his fortune, but another patron accused him of fakery and made him give the money back. A third man bought him a drink. With the bartender, Roughmond got into a conversation in French, and although he walked straight and appeared sober, he also "appeared out of his mind," one customer told the *Stratford Daily Beacon*. Again, he was asked to leave.

Sometime over the noon hour, Roughmond walked across to the police court at City Hall, and when he re-emerged he was wearing a long, black policeman's overcoat. At the Windsor Hotel, he bought a drink and talked nonstop. The bartender thought him out of his mind, the newspapers said. In the early afternoon, at the Mansion House, Roughmond asked for a drink and was refused. When he approached a group of men about reading their palms he was thrown out. Shortly after two o'clock, a number of people saw him heading west along the Huron Road out of town. He walked with a slouch, the witnesses said, and swayed his head from side to side.

Brothers John and George Peake were spreading manure on their fields that afternoon three kilometres west of Stratford and just south of the Huron Road. Around four o'clock, John broke the handle of his manure fork and headed to the barn to fix it, then went all the way to the house to get a drink of sweet cider. His mother had made a fresh batch the previous day and had left a jug at the bottom of the basement steps.

Four people lived in the house, a white-brick building of one and a half storeys. Two daughters had married and moved away, but the two sons still lived there with their parents, William and Mary Peake, both sixty-six years old and married for forty years. That day, William was threshing at a neighbouring farm and Mary was home baking bread and pies.

John entered the kitchen but couldn't see his mother. He called but didn't get an answer. Through a trap door in the kitchen, he started down the cellar steps and in the dim light was startled to see two forms on the brick floor at the bottom. The closest to the steps was a black man lying on his back. The other he assumed must be a black man as well. Quietly, John crept back up the stairs to get his brother. On the way, he checked the orchard and barn for his mother and when he couldn't find her decided she must have gone next door. When he got within earshot he frantically shouted to George about what he saw.

"Get Tom McIntosh," George called back and started running toward the house. McIntosh was ploughing in the next field. As John raced to get him, George reached the house and sneaked down the cellar steps. As his eyes adjusted to the light, he saw the black man and realized the other body was his mother. He could see the man breathing but not her. Terrified, he tiptoed back upstairs and ran to the front gate. John was coming down the road not with McIntosh but with Gordon McNichol.

"It's mother in the cellar and I believe she's dead," George shouted.

Two buggies were driving by, one carrying Robert Fuller and his son James, the other Angus Ballantyne. The men stopped, unhitched their horses, and after a quick huddle George rode off to Stratford to get the police. Robert Fuller picked up a plough rope from his buggy. Together the four men walked around to the back of the house to a woodpile and armed themselves with sticks of wood. McNichol found a pole. They were wondering what to do next when McNichol saw the black man in the kitchen, then at the back door.

"What do you want?" said the man, who turned out to be Roughmond.

"Stop and hold out your hands," Robert Fuller said.

Roughmond hesitated. He looked left and right but, seeing no way past the four men, thrust out his hands. They were streaked with blood. So were his face and clothes.

"I'm innocent," he said as Fuller tied the hands with the rope. "I do not know anything about it."

Stratford police chief John McCarthy walks in step with accused killer Frank Roughmond in front of the jail in an undated photo from 1908 or 1909. Roughmond was found lying next to the body of sixty-six-year-old Mary Peake at the bottom of her cellar stairs.

Three men had drugged him and brought him to the farm, Roughmond said, although numerous witnesses would later tell of seeing him on the road alone.

Once Roughmond's hands and feet were tied, John stayed to guard the prisoner as the others descended the stairs. McNichol went first. When he saw Mary Peake's face covered in blood he fainted, and the others had to carry him back up. Robert Fuller confirmed that Mary Peake was dead. The body was cold, he said. Next to it lay a pair of gold-rimmed glasses, spotted with blood. A threshing gang soon arrived from a nearby farm and threatened to lynch Roughmond from the windmill.

"I am a Canadian," he replied, starting to rant. "There is a King in the Country, and a law above even the King, and there is the man who sells whisky. You can't put a rope about my neck until I'm proved guilty."

The police arrived. Chief John McCarthy drove up in a police wagon with Constable Atchison, who noticed Roughmond was wearing his coat. It had gone missing that morning from the police court. The officers returned to Stratford to question the prisoner, and, calmly smoking his pipe, Roughmond repeated his story about being drugged by three men, robbed of fifteen dollars, and dumped in the Peakes' cellar. Witnesses would later testify that they had seen no evidence of the tramp ever having had fifteen dollars.

At the murder scene, coroner Joseph Monteith examined the slight, frail body. He found bruises to the face, especially around the eyes and mouth, and a broken tooth. The back of the head was so bloodied and lacerated that it might have been smashed against the brick floor, although the skull was not fractured. In the folds of the victim's torn clothing the coroner found a jackknife. It was closed and he found no knife wounds. Instead, he discovered fingermarks around the victim's throat. Mary Peake had been battered, possibly knocked unconscious, raped, and strangled to death.

How Roughmond got into the house and what happened afterward can never be known. Maybe he called at the house for something to eat and while Mary Peake was preparing food for him he attacked her. Maybe he crept downstairs unannounced and attacked her while she was cooking. A row of freshly baked pies sat on a shelf near her body, along with a bowl of bread dough. There had been no struggle, just a violent attack. Her hands were clenched but unmarked.

On May 4, 1909, Roughmond's murder trial opened, Justice William Renwick Riddell of the Ontario Supreme Court presiding. The session lasted two days. Stratford lawyer J.J. Coughlin was assigned to represent the accused. After deliberating for forty-five minutes, the jury found the prisoner guilty, and the judge sentenced him to hang.

Authorities went out of their way to insist that Roughmond had been treated justly, but racial prejudice oozed from their statements.

"You differ from most of us in colour, but no man can say you have not had a fair trial," Justice Riddell said when passing sentence. "Your defence was conducted by Mr. Coughlin, with ability, good taste and perfect judgment, and everything was done for you which the most astute counsel could have done for the largest sum of money."

"Frank Roughmond," the newspapers agreed, "received every legal chance that the bluest-blooded son of Britain had been shown."

Twice after the trial, two psychiatrists examined Roughmond in jail to determine whether he was "weak minded" at the time of the murder. Witnesses might have described him as an incessant talker, incoherent, and "out of his mind," with a way of swaying his head as he walked, but the authorities pronounced him sane.

"We believe that he conforms to the ordinary type of common negro," the psychiatrists wrote, using a now-dated term for "black person," "and is probably a man of brutal instincts; he is also superstitious and ignorant."

At five in the morning on Monday, June 28, 1909, state executioner John Radclive performed his duty in the prison yard at Stratford Jail. Frank Roughmond became the second person executed in Perth County. His body was summarily buried in the prison yard next to Amédée Chattelle, and in 2010 reinterred alongside him at Avondale Cemetery.

To this day, the central mystery of the case remains unanswered. Why was Roughmond found apparently asleep next to the body? Could he really have fallen asleep after such a violent encounter? Did he pass out from drunkenness? Had he fallen down the stairs as he was strangling the woman and knocked himself out? In their rush to a conviction and death sentence, the authorities never let the questions even be asked.

CHAPTER 31
Stratford: Death at Dorothy's Delicatessen

JEAN SATCHELL WAS GROWING UP FAST. She was an out-going, effervescent girl, a teenager with "personality plus," a friend said, bursting to move into the wider world. On completing grade 10, she decided she was finished her studies. For a while, she continued to live with her parents and three younger siblings — a sister and two brothers — on a farm ten kilometres north of Stratford at Gads Hill. She also joined her father's barn-dance band, the Satchell Orchestra, playing piano at community events in and around Perth County. One night she met a man. In October 1952, Reuben Norman walked over and introduced himself at a dance in Wellesley, in neighbouring Waterloo County. She was seventeen; he was twenty-five, a paratrooper in the Royal Canadian Army Service Corps stationed at Camp Borden. The base lay some distance away, near Barrie, but most weekends he visited his parents in the hamlet of Nithburg, not far from Gads Hill.

Jean and Reuben became, in their word, "sweethearts." On week-end visits to his parents' home, Reuben would borrow his father's car and drive to the Satchell farm to see Jean. Her father, Milton Satchell, seemed not to disapprove. He regarded Reuben as "highly intelligent" and "a good young man," and noticed that the solider was not a drinker. "I've seen him refuse a beer," the father said. For Christmas, to demonstrate his affection, Reuben bought Jean a pair of quality leather gloves and told her that, if she ever broke up with him, he would jump and not open his parachute.

By the new year, Jean was again ready for something new. At the beginning of January 1953, she took a job at Harwood's Drug Store in downtown Stratford, on Wellington Street, and moved in with her maternal grandparents on nearby Erie Street. She still visited her parents in Gads Hill, however, and on Saturday, January 24, Reuben came by the farm to see her. Jean told him it was over.

"I heard her tell him she didn't want to see him anymore," her fifteen-year-old sister, Marilyn, later testified.

Reuben Norman, according to his fellow soldiers, never conformed well to Camp Borden. Since enlisting five years earlier, he had shown neither the aptitude nor the discipline for military life.

"The worst soldier of any I knew," Lieutenant Ronald Millikan, his former platoon officer, testified. "I have found Norman inefficient in his work. I would not give him a job of a responsible type.... [He] was a very poor parachutist. It took him longer to learn than anybody else. He was always given a job where it required little mental effort to carry out."

"He never had any close friends — that seemed very odd in the army," Sergeant John Davies said. "He did not have any friends whatsoever."

"The fellows didn't get along with him," said Reuben's brother, Richard, who had served with him on the same base. "He wanted to participate in things but they didn't accept him."

The break-up with Jean devastated Reuben. While visiting Nithburg the following Saturday — January 31 — he borrowed his father's car to drive to Wellesley, and at Louis Mohr's hardware store bought a box of .22-calibre solid-nose bullets.

"Are you going for target practice?" another customer, Clayton Falk, asked him.

"I guess this will finish her up," Reuben said cryptically.

From there he drove to Stratford. Whether he also took a gun with him is not known. He arrived at Jean's grandparents' house at 7:15 in the evening and was shown into the living room, where Jean was lying near a heater to dry her hair. She told him she was going to a movie with her sister, Marilyn, who was visiting.

"Jean and I were going to go to a show," Marilyn said later. "When I finished the dishes I went into the living room and picked up a comic book to read. Jean got up and said she guessed she had better get ready if we were going. She went upstairs and got ready. While I was sitting in the living room, Reuben asked me, 'What's the matter with Jean lately?' I told him I saw no difference, and he said that she was not acting the way she used to do."

When Jean came down the three left the house. Marilyn went ahead, giving her sister and Reuben a moment on the porch. Then Jean caught up and the two girls walked together along Erie Street. Reuben got into his car. When he pulled even with them, he noticed that Jean wasn't wearing the gloves he bought her for Christmas and offered to exchange them if there was a problem.

"Jean answered she would change them herself, and we kept on walking," Marilyn recalled. "When he caught up to us again he called out, 'I'm going out to see your mother and dad.' Then he left."

After the show, Jean walked her sister to the bus station for the trip back to Gads Hill. "That was the last time I saw her," Marilyn said.

Reuben, instead of driving to the Satchell farm that evening, headed back to Nithburg, damaging the car on the way. The next evening, Sunday at six o'clock, his sister Violet passed him in the hallway as she was heading out the door.

"You're happy, aren't you," he said.

She didn't answer but met his eyes. "He looked terrible," she later testified. "He looked as if he hadn't slept."

Violet returned home at around midnight and talked with her brother until two in the morning. "He spoke all about Jean," she recalled. "He was confused that he had lost her. He didn't know why. He kept asking me questions what he should do and whenever I reasoned with him, he just didn't seem to hear me at all. He couldn't figure out why she had changed her mind so quickly. She wanted him before and he couldn't figure out why she had changed."

The next day was Monday, February 2, 1953. Reuben was expected to report for duty at Camp Borden that morning at six o'clock, but he remained at his parents' home in Nithburg. At ten, he opened his brother Stan's fishing-tackle box and took out a German-made Walther semi-automatic, .22-calibre pistol. He was also smoking heavily and borrowed the car to buy cigarettes for himself and his father.

He left the house in full military uniform. He wore a tunic with its Royal Canadian Service Corps insignia, a green military greatcoat, a pair of black paratrooper boots, and a maroon-coloured paratrooper cap. In a coat pocket he carried the pistol. On his return from the store, he placed a package of cigarettes in the mailbox for his father, loaded the gun magazine, and continued to Stratford. He parked near Harwood's Drug Store, located at 22 Wellington Street. The time was twelve noon. He knew that Jean customarily left the store for lunch at that time and walked south toward her grandparents' place. To intercept her, he hid in a doorway down from the drugstore, about where Pizza Bistro is now.

As it happened, Jean was not due for work that day until one. She had forgotten about the shift change, however, and had arrived that morning at eight thirty. When she realized her mistake, rather than return to her grandparents' house, she stayed downtown to shop. By chance, she was walking along Wellington Street carrying a number of parcels at the exact time Reuben was expecting to see her. John Sinclair, who also worked at Harwood's, passed her on his way to lunch.

"She was bubbling over with her usual happiness," he said later. "She did not seem to have a worry in the world."

Over the weekend a winter storm had hit, but shopkeepers had mostly cleared the sidewalk of ice and snow. The street was bustling with people leaving their offices and stepping in and out of stores. Jean was heading south, with the street on her left and the shop doorways to her right. Reuben, still in full uniform, fell into step with her on her right side.

"When she walked by the doorway where I was standing," Reuben wrote in a police statement afterward, "I stepped out and asked if we could have a talk. When she replied 'No' I asked her why she messed things up so bad for me and she replied 'Because I wanted to.' When she did not wish to discuss our past and future I just pulled out the gun and emptied the mag in her body."

Floyd Shrubsole watched it happen. He knew the girl and her family. (Jean's mother was his sister-in-law.) He was parked in front of Dorothy's Delicatessen, at 82 Wellington Street, and was just about to pull away from the curb when he saw Jean coming his way and stopped to offer her a lift.

"I noticed a soldier," Shrubsole later testified.

"What did Jean Marie Satchell do?" the Crown attorney asked.

"Kept walking," he said.

"What did the soldier do?"

"He kept walking beside her," the witness said. "I could see that there were words passed between them."

When they came alongside Dorothy's Delicatessen, in front of his parked car, Shrubsole saw Reuben put his left hand on Jean's right shoulder to slow her down. His right hand then rose out of his greatcoat pocket.

"His right hand came from his side in a motion that appeared he was going to strike her," Shrubsole said. "As soon as his hand came into my view I saw that he had a gun."

Reuben fired three shots into Jean's right side, the muzzle almost flush to her coat. She screamed, spun around to the left, away from Reuben and toward the street, and staggered backward toward the shops, dropping her parcels and falling to the icy sidewalk.

"She screamed then fell," said Edith Candler, a clerk in a nearby bakeshop.

As the girl buckled, Reuben fired three more shots into her chest and abdomen, for a total of six, then started to reload.

Coming out of Sage's grocery store a few metres away, eighteen-year-old Alan Jones heard the gunshots and rushed toward them. He dropped to his knees on the sidewalk and ran his arm under Jean's head and shoulders, lifting her from the snow.

Shot And Killed On City Street

Photo by Meyers Studio

MORTALLY WOUNDED on Wellington st. here, Monday noon, 17-year-old Miss Jean Marie Satchell, a clerk in a Stratford drug store and daughter of Mr. and Mrs. Milton Satchell, R.R. 2 Gadshill, died a few minutes later on her way to the operating room of the Stratford General Hospital.

The girl with "personality plus," seventeen-year-old Jean Satchell, appears in a family photo at the top of page one of the *Stratford Beacon Herald* on February 3, 1953. The image here was copied from microfilm.

"Somebody call a doctor," he shouted.

Reuben, standing directly over him, fired three more times at the girl's face. "She won't need a doctor now," he said.

Reuben turned. He walked back up the street, northward, and veered toward the police station at the back of City Hall. He moved at a pace between a walk and a run, or what soldiers call "on the double."

At the same time, two police officers ran out of the station. Inspector Joseph Taylor had been putting on his coat for lunch when he heard the first shots, and detective Mark Anthony followed him out the door. Reuben advanced toward them carrying the gun in his right hand, waist high, with the barrel pointed straight at Taylor. Reuben wore "a set expression," Taylor said. He walked "like a well-trained soldier," Anthony said. The officers, however, never wavered. When Taylor got close, he swung out of the line of fire and snatched the gun from Reuben's hand.

"Okay, okay, you can have it," Reuben said, releasing his grip.

Anthony grabbed him and handed him to Taylor, then raced toward the crowd gathered around the fallen girl.

"I stooped down and took her hand to see if there was any pulse," the detective later testified. "There was but she was very pale. Somebody offered me a blanket and I put it over her."

By then, Dr. Alexander Sinclair, from nearby Sebringville, had exited one of the stores to attend to the girl. "Her pupils were fully dilated," he said. Her pulse was "fairly good." With Detective Anthony on the scene, the doctor left to phone an ambulance and alert the Stratford General Hospital emergency room. Then he drove to the hospital himself.

Inside the police station, Reuben took off his greatcoat and draped it over a railing. Keys fell out of one of his pockets. "The keys to the old man's car," he said. "I smashed it up on Saturday night and she was the cause of it."

Inspector Taylor rifled through Reuben's pockets and found forty rounds of ammunition. "He didn't show any signs of fear," Taylor said. "I would say he appeared relieved, like a man who had got something off his chest. His speech was very clear and distinct."

"He was calm and cool," said constable Arthur Nickles, who was also there.

When Detective Anthony returned from the crime scene, he told the prisoner he would be charged with "shooting with intent." Then the telephone rang. Inspector Taylor picked up the receiver and put it down again. "The girl is dead," he said. At the hospital, Dr. Sinclair had pronounced her dead on arrival. "The charge is now murder," Anthony said.

Taylor cautioned the prisoner that he did not need to say anything, but that anything he did say would be taken down in writing and used as evidence. Reuben said he would like to make a statement. "Where's the typewriter?" he said.

Given a desk and typewriter, Reuben wound a statement sheet through the rollers and, in a space provided for the criminal charge, typed "Murder." For the next half hour, he sat chain-smoking and composing a confession, beginning from the time he left his parents' house at ten that morning, to the moment he handed the gun to Inspector Taylor.

"I just pulled out the gun and emptied the mag in her body," he typed.

At his trial that May, three months after the murder, Reuben pleaded "not guilty." His defence was mental illness and the jury found him unfit to stand trial by reason of insanity. At a hospital for the criminally insane in Penetanguishene, however, doctors determined that he was not mentally ill after all. That November, a second jury also deemed him fit, and at the trial that began immediately, a third jury found him guilty of capital murder. Reuben insisted he did not feel culpable.

"It is true," he told the court, "that the events took place at my hand." But, he also said, "within my own heart I have no sense of guilt.... I was mentally ill and I am cured of mental illness."

Just after midnight, on February 18, 1954, one year and two weeks after he shot Jean Satchell to death on Wellington Street during the lunch-hour rush, Reuben Norman walked soldier-like across the courtyard of Stratford Jail to the scaffold. He was dressed the way he had dressed for his trial, in a dark blue suit, white shirt, and dark bow tie.

"I offered myself to my country and now am called to a greater service," the condemned man told a handful of officials. "I realize I'm an undue burden on you people called to witness my execution, and I ask God to bless you all."

In the end, Reuben Norman offered no word of remembrance for his former teenage sweetheart, who, "bubbling over with her usual happiness," simply wished to make her own way in the world.

CHAPTER 32
Millbank: Kitchen Table Clairvoyant

TWO MEN ARRIVED in Millbank to inquire about a friend who had disappeared. "Where is he?" they asked. With her answer, Vera McNichol established herself as a Perth County folk legend.

"He's dead," the short, grey-haired woman told the men at her kitchen table, thumbing through playing cards. "He is covered up and I don't like what I see. Everything is [motionless] around him and he is down deep in the ground ... near his home. Maybe somebody has dug a trench."

The missing man was Angus Tuer. He was thirty-three years old, last seen a couple of weeks earlier, on December 10, 1973. The Tuer family owned and operated four contiguous farms outside Mitchell, twenty kilometres northwest of Stratford. Angus lived with his mother, Stella, on what they called the "home farm." His older brother, William, lived nearby.

There were just three people in the family. The father had died nearly twenty years earlier. William had run the business into receivership, after which Angus had taken control and put William on a salary, an arrangement the elder brother resented. A third brother, Edmund, had died in a car accident out West and had left a loaded handgun in the barn.

About seven o'clock in the evening on January 23, 1974 — a month and a half after Angus's disappearance — four men sat together in Mitchell's Royal Hotel drinking lounge. They decided to drive to Angus Tuer's farm to look for the body. Whether they knew of Vera McNichol's vision they never made clear. In any case, after searching abandoned silos in the dark without success, they came across an old, unused well.

"I saw something [at the bottom] that looked like a big bran bag," one of the searchers said later.

The next morning, police recovered Angus's body with one end of a chain around his neck and the other end attached to a car transmission.

A news reporter who knew of McNichol's revelation phoned her for comment and she improved on her original prognosis. "I said [the dead man] would be down in something, possibly a ditch, trench, or well," she said.

"Seer Had Suggested Man Perhaps in Well," the headline read.

Besides being thrown down the well with a weight around his neck, Angus had also been shot in the forehead with, it turned out, Edmund's handgun from the barn. Ten months later, a jury found William Tuer guilty of murdering his younger brother out of jealousy and a wish to regain control of the farm. The killer went to prison for life, and McNichol's reputation as a psychic soared.

The seer was born in 1910 in Glen Allan, not far from Millbank. She trained as a nurse in Listowel, worked at a hospital in Peterborough, married a Listowel farmer, and moved with him into an 1847 two-storey house in Millbank that had served variously as a stagecoach stop, general store, and hotel. By the 1960s, word was getting around about her special gift.

"I had my first vision when I was nine years old," she told a *Stratford Beacon Herald* reporter in 1967. "My mother had a friend, with her foster child, visiting her, and when I looked at them, I told the friend that she and the child would die together within a week. My mother's friend said this couldn't be possible, as the child was going in a new home shortly. My father was furious with me, and sent me to bed without any supper. My mother was not surprised, because she was gifted with second sight, although she didn't practise it. Two days later my mother's friend and the child were killed on the highway, near New Hamburg."

At her home in 1976, Millbank folk hero Vera McNichol works a deck of regular playing cards to enhance her psychic powers. Her reputation soared with her pronouncements on the disappearance of Mitchell-area farmer Angus Tuer.

In subsequent interviews, McNichol repeated the story, sometimes recalling herself as three years old instead of nine, sometimes as two. People hearing of her powers would sometimes drive long distances to seek her out. She had no telephone and no appointment book. People would arrive and sometimes find a lineup of a dozen cars. In good weather visitors waited outside on chairs and a bench, and in foul weather they waited in their cars. Many knew to bring a lunch. A rickety outhouse stood not far away. When their turn came, visitors would enter a back door, walk through a woodshed, and be welcomed into the kitchen, where McNichol would be sitting at a table with a dog-eared set of ordinary playing cards that she used to help make predictions. The room had only one light. Women generally asked advice about men — boyfriends or husbands, she said. Men usually asked about business matters.

"Everything is performed over the kitchen table," the *Beacon Herald* reported in 1976. "The room itself is heated by a wood stove. It's dimly lit, hot and smells slightly acrid with burning wood and grease. The wall paper is smoke-stained and peeling and the floor is patch-worked with different patterns of worn tile."

Whether or not she was clairvoyant, McNichol possessed a natural empathy for people and a rare ability to listen. Sometimes parents would bring a delinquent youngster. McNichol would speak to the child alone to "help them by uplifting them," she once said. "Never preach to a child. Help them by trying to understand them."

She would never rush people. Visits generally lasted an hour or more, which is why people had to wait so long in line, and they would come away feeling as though she was a long-time friend. Her powers of concentration seemed boundless. Visiting hours sometimes lasted from five in the morning until midnight, and people described her as perpetually cheerful. In her nursing days people called her "Sunshine." She often giggled. Her husband, John, apparently never complained about the demands she put on herself and often played checkers in the parlour with people waiting their turn.

Although she never charged a fee for a consultation, people would generally buy one of her books as compensation. She wrote more than thirty books and booklets over the years, all self-published, including children's stories of the Bible, five volumes of autobiography, and numerous Perth County histories. Many entries she wrote in verse — simple child-like poems written with no particular artistry or ear for rhythm. One was titled "Jessie Keith," and began:

The brutal murder of Jessie Keith,
Has been sadly told and re-told,
The gruesome facts about the case,
Would make one's blood turn cold.

A few inaccuracies appear in the poem. Jessie buys rice in town, not pot barley. The school friend who walks her to the railway tracks from town is not Edith Lephardt but Elizabeth Mitchell (who married to become Mrs. Ezra Biehn). William Travis appears in the poem as "John Travis." Armour Laird appears as "Joe Laird." Chattelle was seen "eating turnip in a farmer's field," the poem says, instead of using a knife with his left hand to cut pieces of turnip as Travis walked him along the tracks to Cataract. However unreliable the details, McNichol writes with affection and never succumbs to sentimentality. In her closing lines, she expresses the view that society dealt with Chattelle in the only way it could.

He was identified by Johnson Kidd,
Mrs. Cattell, H. Leslie and Joe Laird.
On May 31st, 1895, he was hanged,
Such men as he, could not be spared.

In 1988, McNichol moved to a nursing home in Brunner and died seven years later at the age of eighty-five. Her husband predeceased her. The McNichol house was to be demolished, but a hairdresser from London, Ontario, bought it and moved it across the street onto a new foundation. In 1990, Bill and Sharon Wreford, owners of the upscale Bradshaws home décor and kitchenware shop in Stratford, purchased it. First they used it as a weekend home, then as their principal residence. They undertook a total renovation. Across the back they added two full-length balconies. To the side they added a tastefully coherent extension that includes a main entrance, a spacious dining area, and a well-equipped modern kitchen. McNichol would hardly recognize the place.

In 2011, the Wrefords sold the house to a married couple from Waterloo, Geoff Schmitt and Jennifer Nicholson.

The original portion of Vera McNichol's house, a former stagecoach inn, peeks through the trees on the banks of Millbank's Nith River. Renovations and additions have transformed the home into a residence the late clairvoyant would scarcely recognize.

"People ask, 'Is the house haunted?'" Nicholson says. "I tell them, 'No, it's full of positive energy.'"

She gave me a tour. In the former parlour, she pulled back a carpet to show me marks where the nineteenth-century hotel bar once stood. It serves now as a spectacular kitchen counter. The room where McNichol counselled visitors is divided into a small library and bathroom. The only presence that might be said to haunt the place would be Bill Wreford, the previous owner. He moved back to Stratford but sometimes drives by to reflect on the twenty-five years he and his wife, now deceased, spent together in the house.

"If I see him I flag him down," Nicholson says. "He and Sharon did a fabulous job making this a home. I tell him, 'You're always welcome here.'"

Of the thousands of people — some estimates run to 250,000 — who consulted Vera McNichol over the years, many retain fond memories of their visit. One is Richard Houghton. In 1981, he lit out on a road trip in an old Volvo station wagon from Red Deer College, Alberta, with two friends, Kathy Lang and Gary Elger, a.k.a. "Drifter," "a poet, musician, painter, and part-time anarchist." They were on their Christmas vacation. They arrived early in the day at Millbank, drank beer and smoked cigarettes for breakfast, and approached the old McNichol house before a lineup formed.

"Knocking on the kitchen door in the darkness we were startled by a huge old man with fingers like sausages," Houghton recalled in 1994 for the *Edmonton Journal*. "Gruffly, he said we might as well come in, and [we] were shown into the dimly lit kitchen. Vera, in black dress and shawl, greeted us warmly, offered a cup of tea, and quickly began telling our fortunes with a deck of cards. The fortunes we scribbled down that day seemed mysterious and wonderful. I don't have that piece of paper any more, and couldn't remember 15 minutes later what Vera had said. But I do remember that we would all be granted our wishes and that great adventures were in store."

McNichol turned out to be right in two of the three cases. Elger's fortune she got wrong. Three years after the visit he was murdered at a party in Red Deer. Houghton's wish came true. He wanted to become a journalist and landed a job with the *Edmonton Journal*. Kathy Lang did even better. Four years after the visit, she won Canada's top music prize, a Juno Award, for most promising Canadian female vocalist, under the name k.d. lang. Four years after that, she shared a Grammy Award with Roy Orbison for their duet "Crying," establishing herself as an international star.

ANNA MAE'S BAKERY

A thriving commercial centre in Chattelle's day, Millbank is regionally famous now for Anna Mae's Bakery, a sprawling restaurant seating nearly two hundred people. It is often packed. I arrived on a Thursday in July at half past noon and waited half an hour for a table.

Anna Mae Wagler started small. In 1978, she baked pies in her kitchen and sold them at the end of her laneway. In 1991, she opened a bakery and small café at the present location on Perth Line 72, which runs through town. She and her family lived in an adjoining house. Bit by bit she expanded into her living room, dining room, and finally into the bedrooms, which is why the restaurant consists of so many distinct spaces. In 2001 she sold the place, but subsequent owners hold to tradition. Anna Mae's Bakery still serves home-style Mennonite meals of meat, potatoes, and freshly baked pie. The signature dish is "broasted chicken" — marinated, seasoned chicken cooked in a pressure fryer.

E&E'S CLOTH & CREATIONS

E&E are husband and wife Edgar and Emmaline Wagler, founders in 1990 of a fabrics business catering to quilt-makers. It occupies the original general store in Newton, a crossroads four kilometres west of present-day Millbank. Originally, Newton was called Millbank station, a stop midway between Stratford and Palmerston on the Stratford and Huron Railway. When news reports of the Jessie Keith murder mentioned Millbank station, they meant Newton. The tracks ran within metres of the general store, meaning that Amédée Chattelle would also have walked within metres of it.

Emmaline Wagler stands outside her textile shop, E&E's Cloth & Creations, housed in Newton's original general store. Amédée Chattelle would have walked right by it on his way to Listowel.

207

A mural on one side of E&E's handsome yellow-brick building depicts a rural scene, painted some years ago by a high school class from Listowel. "Newton founded in 1881," an inscription says. "A small town … with a big heart." Hay bales lie in the field, a quilt hangs from a line, a farmhouse and barn stand in the distance, and in the foreground a man steers his horse and buggy down a dirt road. The mural is not meant to show the past. An orange-and-red triangle on the back of the buggy, alerting motorists to a slow-moving vehicle, indicates a present-day rig driven by a member of the Old Order Amish.

CHAPTER 33
Listowel: The Jessie Keith
Memorial Tour

THE KEITH FARMHOUSE

The former Keith property is numbered 5588 on the north side of an unpaved country road called Line 84, but nothing remains of the old farmhouse. Farther along, on the same side, stands a chicken farm, and beyond that a field that rises to the spot where the killer first attacked Jessie on the railway tracks. One summer Sunday morning, the farmer who now works the land, Eric Haverkamp, kindly walked me across the field. The tracks are gone, the fence over which the killer hauled her is gone, and the swampy wood is reduced to a patch of bush some distance away. All that remains from the fateful day, Haverkamp pointed out, are the remnants of nineteenth-century drainage pipes, like one that created the pool where Chattelle washed the blood off his hands.

THE KINSMEN TRAIL

On the day of her death, Jessie followed the train tracks into Listowel and returned the same way. For anybody heading into town today, the former railway bed becomes visible on the other side of Tremaine Avenue South as a recreation trail for hiking, cycling, and cross-country skiing. Jessie turned right at Wallace Avenue South, formerly Mill Street, and walked past the Town Hall, which would have been on her right, to Main Street and the downtown shops. On her return, she walked directly past the hall again with her friend Edith Lephardt. They parted at the railway crossing.

THE TOWN HALL

Today the Town Hall is a chiropractic clinic. Nothing about the building at 170 Wallace Avenue South alludes to the drama that took place on October 26, 1894, when a thousand angry people, a number equal to half the town's population, met the hackney carriage carrying the suspected killer to the coroner's inquest. "Hang him! Get the rope!" cried the crowd, and the coroner, Dr. James Rankin, opened the Town Hall doors to as many spectators as could fit.

Rainclouds gather above the former Listowel Town Hall as if to evoke the drama of coroner James Rankin's inquest on Friday, October 26, 1894.

LIVINGSTONE MANOR

The *e* in *Livingstone* is a mistake. John Livingston, with no *e*, built this stately mansion in 1880 while overseeing the Listowel flax growing and manufacturing operations for J. & J. Livingston, the biggest flax enterprise in North America. During Jessie Keith's lifetime, growing and milling flax counted as one of Listowel's most important businesses, and John Livingston was buried the same day Jessie's memorial statue was unveiled.

Three generations of Livingstons continued to occupy the manor at 480 Main Street West after John's death. In 1951, the family sold the house to a funeral company, which later sold it to a couple as a private residence. In 1987, the building became the upscale retirement residence that can be seen today.

John Livingstone, with an *e*, had nothing to do with the manor but lived in Listowel at the same time, hence the confusion. He was the elder brother of the great missionary and Nile River explorer, Dr. David Livingstone. The missionary's brother arrived in Canada from Scotland in 1840, and enjoyed success as a Listowel farmer and later as the town druggist. He retired in 1873 and left his drugstore at Main and Wallace Streets to his son. On the day she was killed, Jessie would have passed Livingstone's Drug Store twice on her errands.

Cherubs frolic amid the new growth of spring in a brightly painted mural above a doorway inside Livingstone Manor, built in 1880 by "flax king" John Livingston. He hired Hungarian-born artist Karl Muller to decorate the interior in linseed-oil-based paints.

THE IMPERIAL HOTEL

Like Livingstone Manor, the building across the street at 469 Main Street West is now a retirement home. On May 21, 1896, however, it was the hotel where John Livingston suddenly put his hand to his chest in severe pain. Twenty minutes later he was dead of a heart attack. Earlier, the structure had been known as the Last Chance Hotel, the last opportunity for travellers to get a drink before heading west out of town.

THE HORATIO WALKER HOME

At 555 Main Street West, half a block from the former Imperial Hotel, stands one of Listowel's most historically significant homes. Today it is called Hardwood Haven Bed and Breakfast, run by Ty and Fay Cross.

In 1852, John Binning erected a log house on the site and became Listowel's first settler. In 1860, Thomas Walker and his wife, originally from Yorkshire, England, built what is now the back part of the house when their son Horatio was two years old. The boy was born in Listowel and he spent his early childhood here. When he was thirteen, the family moved to Rochester, New York, and later Toronto, where Horatio eventually launched his career as an artist, celebrated especially for his scenes of rural Quebec. In 1877, a new owner named George Towner built a substantial addition with a distinctive four-storey belvedere.

The house next door, at 517 Main Street West, is believed to be Listowel's first brick home, likely dating to the 1870s. Typical of the period, its front door is centred under a gable and leads to a central hall.

LISTOWEL TRAIN STATION

Although the station of 1894 is gone, the building that replaced it is now of historic value and has been renovated as the meeting hall for the Listowel Kinsmen Club. The address is 555 Binning Street West, the spot where Listowel townsfolk angrily swarmed Amédée Chattelle when he was first arrested, then showered him with silver coins. This is also where Chattelle boarded the train for Stratford after the coroner's inquest, where police chief John McCarthy nearly fell under the rolling train wheels, and where his brother, constable Thomas McCarthy, waved a loaded revolver over his head to quiet the crowd.

LISTOWEL CLOCK TOWER

When Jessie Keith picked up the newspapers for her father, she did so at the general store owned by W.H. Hacking, Listowel's first postmaster. He ran the post office, sold seeds and schoolbooks, issued marriage licences, and rented accommodation to newly married couples. Over the years, his business relocated several times due to fire and other circumstances, but in 1894 it almost certainly stood on Main Street West, just past what is now Hardwood Haven Bed and Breakfast, the former Horatio Walker home. On her last walk, Jessie would have covered almost the length of Main Street West, past John Livingston's house and other landmarks.

To the people of Listowel, "the old post office" is not the Hacking post office but a grand building opened in 1911 at Main Street West and Argyle Street. When it was torn down in 1982, many people missed its presence. In 1994, to help fill the void, a replica of the building's landmark clock tower went up in a municipal parkette where Elizabeth Street crosses Wallace Avenue North. Local jewellers Neil and Tim Bakelaar, father and son respectively, restored the original clock for the tower, and Tim still keeps it running.

FAIRVIEW CEMETERY

Once, when I was visiting Jessie's memorial, a husband and wife approached on their bicycles, the husband pulling a trailer with a toddler in the back.

"Oh, that's where we're going, too," the woman said when she saw me approach the Goddess of Flora. She introduced herself as Jaime Sharpin and said she likes to visit Jessie's grave. "I grew up on Reserve Street, which went onto the railway tracks," she said of the street a little east of Mill Street, or Wallace Avenue South. "It was always said that Jessie walked home from school there, and we used to play there, so I've always known about her. When I was in high school, the Black Door Theatre drama club also did a play about her."

A statue of the Roman Goddess of Flora, scaled to the size of a thirteen-year-old girl, looks down on Jessie's grave in Fairview Cemetery, Listowel. Speaking at the monument's unveiling in 1896, secularist leader William Algie called the girl's murder "the saddest day in the history of this community."

A legend about the statue also circulated in those days, Sharpin recalled. "It was said that the statue once had ruby eyes and that if you stared into them you could see the whole murder play out," she said.

The cemetery is at 875 Davidson Avenue North and the statue remains one of its tallest and most distinguishing features. From the main gates, walk straight to the first laneway, turn left, and continue to midway down the first block. The statue is on the left, shaded by a tree canopy. If you were to instead turn right and climb a slight rise, you would come to a massive gravestone marked "Livingston," where John Livingston was buried the day Jessie's memorial statue was unveiled.

The goddess of flowers, springtime, and youth extends her hand as if casting a rose on Jessie's grave. Although weathered, the marble statue remains a work of exquisite tenderness, a figure of enduring grace and beauty to mark one of the ugliest episodes in Perth County history.

CHAPTER 34
The End of the Line

THE ELORA CATARACT TRAILWAY

A recreational trail now follows the final forty-two kilometres of Amédée Chattelle's intended escape route. It features the spectacular Elora Gorge at one end and the stunning Forks of the Credit Provincial Park at the other, on the Niagara Escarpment. Between the two points lie expansive cornfields and horse pastures, punctuated by rural villages. In its entirety, the path runs forty-seven kilometres along the former Credit Valley Railway bed. Chattelle, however, joined it at Fergus. He followed the train tracks from Palmerston straight into Fergus, bypassing Elora, and from there continued to Cataract.

One summer weekend I cycled the trailway. From Toronto, I took a GO bus to Guelph and followed bicycle paths and country roads to Elora and almost to Fergus, stopping to tour the former House of Industry and Refuge, or "poorhouse," now a national historic site and museum. The next day I rejoined the trailway and rode to Cataract. As I pedalled, I tried to imagine Chattelle's emotional torment as he strived to make headway in the late-October cold. I saw nothing left of Belwood station, where in 1894 grain dealer James Goodall spotted the killer, or of Hillsburgh station, where James Collins called "hello" and in return Chattelle "made no response or motion."

In Erin, the most substantial of the villages beyond Fergus, I took the self-guided walking tour beginning at Main Street and the West Credit River, where a plaque tells of Erin's founding in 1820. Highlights include the Busholme Inn, built in 1886 as a hospital and now open as a pub. Signs on many of Main Street's shops and businesses also give historic details of the buildings. Nothing, however, remains of the station where, almost exactly three days after the killing, baggage handler William Travis eyed Chattelle approaching along the tracks and said, "That's a pretty hard-looking seed."

Six and a half kilometres farther on, I arrived at Cataract, end of the line for Chattelle but a gateway now for Bruce Trail hikers into the Forks of the Credit Provincial Park. The former Dew Drop Inn of Chattelle's time, originally built as a post office in 1855, now functions as a boutique hotel and yoga retreat, the Forks of the Credit Inn.

ELORA AND FERGUS

Together, these two villages today make a popular getaway for urban dwellers. Chattelle never saw Elora, but he did wander into downtown Fergus. Shortly before five o'clock on the day after the killing, witnesses spotted him on the St. David Street Bridge. He would have been standing between two landmark structures, both of which have been recently renovated.

One is the Marshall Block, built in 1883 by John Black, a successful grain merchant and cattle dealer. Fashioned from brown sandstone hauled from the Credit Valley to the east, it stands out from the primarily limestone streetscape. One corner is angled at forty-five degrees to face the intersection and rises as an octagonal stone tower. The corner entrance opens to the popular Vault Coffee and Espresso Bar, so named because a branch of the Imperial Bank of Canada once occupied the space. Customers can sit in the former vault to drink their coffee.

On the other side of the bridge, Chattelle would have seen the formidable limestone complex functioning then as the Beatty Brothers Farm Implement factory. Today, the buildings house shops and restaurants under the collective name Fergus Marketplace on the River.

A pedestrian waits to cross in front of the 1883 Marshall Block, built in downtown Fergus from Credit Valley sandstone by grain merchant and cattle dealer John Black. It is one of two heritage sites on either side of the St. David Street Bridge.

THE VILLAGE DUO

Former stage actor Gary Bryant and banjo player Alvin Koop have been giving historic walking tours of Elora and Fergus for more than seventeen years. Calling themselves "the Village Duo," they dress in period costume and portray local historic figures. Many of the tours are free, coordinated with such festivals as Doors Open, Culture Days, and the signature Fergus Scottish Festival and Highland Games. At Halloween, the two guides give ghost walks and "lantern tours."

In Fergus, one of their most surprising stops is at a large granite rock, or stane, left by an ancient glacier. *Stane* is a Scottish word for *stone*. This one sits in the middle of what was once Fergus's town square, James Square, named after village co-founder James Webster. Children called the rock the "castle stane" because they played "King of the Castle" on it. Young couples called it the "kissing stane" because to be kissed while seated on the rock was supposed to bring good luck.

"It is rare [in nineteenth-century Ontario] that young people would influence a whole town," Koop and Bryant tell their tour groups, "but it

Gary Bryant, left, and Alvin Koop, performing as "the Village Duo," lead a walking tour that includes the "kissing stane," a granite rock deposited during the ice age. Bryant wears a "Christy" hat of the type Amédée Chattelle wore on his way to Listowel.

became tolerated that young couples could show open public affection here. Not on the streets, not anywhere else, but here."

Near the stone, the local business association has today installed a Love Lock sculpture, to which sweethearts can affix a padlock symbolizing their commitment to each other.

THE NOTORIOUS JANE LEWIS

Between Elora and Fergus stands a great building on a hill. The poorest of the poor once lived there. "The House of Industry and Refuge" authorities formally named it, but everybody else called it "the poorhouse." Built in 1877 of limestone cut from the banks of the Grand River below, and surrounded by barns, outbuildings, and tilled fields, it housed people who had become destitute — mostly through no fault of their own. They had been injured on the job, or grown old and disabled, or become mentally infirm, or their husband had died and left children to feed. They were the "deserving poor" — deserving of help but without the extended family to

A bride and her attendants cross the lawn of an institution that once housed the poorest of the poor, the Wellington County House of Industry and Refuge. It functions now as a museum and national historic site.

provide it. Faced with no alternative, they accepted to be institutionalized in what proved to be an early attempt at a provincial social safety net.

The building still stands halfway between Elora and Fergus, twenty kilometres north of Guelph. It is a museum now and national historic site, a reminder of what was once a chain of such shelters across the province. Amédée Chattelle passed within sight of it. Shortly after four o'clock the day after he killed Jessie Keith, somebody spotted him on the tracks nearby.

One of the building's residents at the time was Jane Lewis, referred to by a museum panel now as "the notorious Jane Lewis." She had arrived at the institution from Guelph in 1878, one year after it opened. Earlier, she had been known for her sinewy strength, and the way she could unload wagons and sling crates as ably as a husky man. She was also a heavy drinker and smoker, however, who had eventually resorted to begging in the streets. On the steps of the poorhouse she must have looked drastically diminished, because the admissions officer guessed her to be seventy-five years old. She was forty-two. Her real name was not Jane Lewis but Jane Ward, and she had once been the central figure in a famous Toronto murder.

The victim was John Sheridan Hogan. He was one of Toronto's most prominent citizens — a tall, agile, dashing figure of forty-four with many powerful friends. From humble beginnings in Ireland, he had immigrated to Canada as a boy of twelve. He had become a lawyer, then a journalist. By late 1859, he had left his job as editor-in-chief of the *Toronto Colonist* and was serving as a Member of Parliament in the pre-Confederation Province of Canada. His acquaintances included fellow parliamentarians George Brown, founder of the *Toronto Globe*, and John A. Macdonald, attorney general and later Canada's first prime minister.

Married but separated, Hogan lived by himself at Rossin House, a five-storey luxury hotel with gas lighting and steam heating at King and York Streets. On December 1, 1859, he was visiting his mistress, Sarah Lawrie, a single mother of three who lived nearby on Nelson Street. At 8:30, he decided to leave Lawrie's place, stop by the *Colonist* office, then visit a colleague on the east side of the Don River, outside the city limits. It was well after dark and Lawrie suggested he not go. He didn't listen.

"Watch out for the Brook's Bush Gang," she said.

"I'm sure they won't hurt me," he replied.

Hogan was known for his irregular habits, and when he failed to return to Rossin House few people voiced concern. When he still hadn't surfaced after a couple of months, however, the government posted a five hundred dollar reward for information. Wild stories circulated in the press. He had moved to Buffalo, committed suicide, absconded to Texas or Australia, been admitted to a lunatic asylum in Cincinnati, or been thrown over Niagara Falls.

On March 30, 1861, sixteen months after his disappearance, four duck hunters spotted a body at the mouth of the Don River. The upper portions of the corpse were badly decomposed, making identification difficult. The coat pockets were torn and empty. A tailor identified the garment as one he had made for Hogan, and a leather worker similarly recognized the enameled sealskin boots he had custom-designed for the politician. Lawrie noticed that the big toes on the corpse were longer than the second toes, just like Hogan's. Repairs to the shirt collar were ones she had made, she said, and she identified a pin she had used to tighten the waistband of Hogan's flannel underwear the night before his disappearance.

Suspicion fell on the Brook's Bush Gang. It was a loose collection of thieves, drunkards, and prostitutes based east of the Don River, in a large wooded area centred around an old barn and abandoned outbuildings. Little else was known about the troublemakers. Estimates of their numbers ranged from fifteen to forty. Seeking a lead in the case, Toronto police detective James Colgan called at a clapboard house in a poor section of the city looking for Ellen McGillick, a known gang affiliate.

Newspapers later described her as a tall, strapping twenty-three-year-old. "She is a finely-developed, well-built girl with a carriage of some grace," the *Toronto Leader* said. Six months earlier, when Colgan had arrested her in connection with the theft of a watch, she had pulled a knife and stabbed him in the chest. She had not caused serious injury, however, and Colgan had declined to charge her with attempted murder. Afterward she had begun volunteering information on the Brook's Bush Gang. In the Hogan case, in return for immunity from prosecution, she told the detective everything.

On the night of December 1, 1859, McGillick said, she crossed the wooden Don River Bridge at Queen Street. With her were Jane Ward and other male and female members of the Brook's Bush Gang, including James Brown and John Sherrick. As they reached the city side of the bridge, they saw Hogan approaching. He was on friendly terms with some of the group. As a newspaperman, he had often visited the jail and given the prisoners spare change, and although he had previously been stopped on the bridge he had never been harmed.

Two of the women, McGillick and Ward, spoke to Hogan. Ward then took him by the arm and walked him to the bridge. At the railing she asked him for money. When he reached for a roll of bills, she snatched it from him, and when he tried to snatch it back, three men jumped him. Ward slung a stone in a handkerchief and struck him on the head. Maybe the blow killed him, or maybe Hogan was still alive. In any case, the gang rifled through his clothes for valuables, tied a weight around his feet, and tossed him over the handrail.

"God damn him, fling him over," Ward shouted.

By then, McGillick was sitting on the east side of the bridge. When she saw the men throw Hogan into the water, she screamed, and Ward walked up and punched her in the face. "The man I struck with that [stone] will never tell another tale," Ward said.

McGillick decided not return that night to the bush. Instead, she headed into town, and a Constable Gibben, who passed her, later testified to seeing "blood on her face, clothes, and hands" and looking "as if she had been in a row."

The next day, McGillick went back to the bridge with James Brown and John Sherrick. They spotted blood on the railing and Brown chipped much of it off with a penknife.

To the detective, and later in court, McGillick said Ward delivered the blow to Hogan's head and three men dumped the body: Brown, Sherrick, and Hugh McEntameny. In the months since the murder McEntameny had died. Police arrested Ward and Brown, and located Sherrick in Kingston Penitentiary, where he was serving time for robbery. Fourteen other Brook's Bush members were also rounded up and charged as accessories after the fact.

The first gang members to stand trial were Ward and Sherrick. A defence witness testified that Sherrick was chopping wood north of Toronto on the night in question, a flimsy-sounding alibi but difficult to disprove.

Attention shifted to Ward. She had been born in Yorkshire, England, and had immigrated with her family at the age of four to the Hamilton area, where her parents were still farming. For the past four or five years, she had been engaged in "crime and shame," the papers said, and had served time for robbery. Ward's eyes, the *Leader* said, had "a peculiar glitter denoting a vicious and revengeful nature." She was twenty-three years old but even then must have looked older, as the *Globe* suggested:

> She is about twenty-five years of age, tall, and well made. Her features are regular, and were it not that disease and dissipation have left their marks on her face, she would be considered a "good looking woman." She is very passionate

and vindictive, and has long ruled the members of the gang, both men and women. All alike feared her when her blood was up. She is much addicted to the use of intoxicating liquor and has frequently figured in our Police reports as a drunken and disorderly character. She has several times been "up" for robbery and larceny, but has generally managed to escape punishment and been acquitted.

When McGillick took the witness stand, Ward let loose a rambling curse. "Oh, Lord God in Heaven, this day send down on Ellen McGillock, and if I am guilty may God punish me, and if you are guilty of the false oath you have taken, may God bring it down this day," she said. "Oh, Ellen McGillock, you will never get over this as long as you live. Oh, Lord in Heaven — "

After a two-day trial, the jury delivered their verdict. "Both not guilty," the foreman said.

The jury had accepted Sherrick's alibi. They acquitted Ward perhaps out of an aversion to seeing a woman hang, the papers said.

The trial judge, chief justice Sir John Beverley Robinson, one of the province's most powerful men, scolded her. "I would say to you," he told Ward, "that the sooner you abandon the disreputable life you have been leading, the better."

James Brown went on trial alone. He declared his innocence. He did not see Hogan that night, he said, he didn't scrape blood off the railing the next day, and he didn't even hear about the events until later. Witnesses other than McGillick, however, had seen him on the bridge on the night of the murder, including Dr. T.C. Gamble, a venerable city physician. Brown objected, saying the doctor had never seen him before, but Gamble said he knew Brown by his disfigured, cancerous nose. "Anyone who has seen that nose of yours is not likely to forget it," the doctor said.

The jury found Brown guilty of capital murder. He appealed, but a second trial confirmed the verdict, and on March 10, 1862, five thousand people gathered at the Toronto Jail to watch him hang. It was Toronto's last public execution.

Afterward the Brook's Bush Gang dispersed. Jane Ward's subsequent movements went undocumented, but at some point she ended up in Guelph and then at the poorhouse, under the name Jane Lewis. In 1878, only months after she was admitted, a reporter from the *Elora Lightning Express* toured the institution and wrote a glowing review of the place but not of her. The bedrooms were clean, the bedding comfortable, the ventilation pleasing, and the clothes sewn on the premises made of warm, quality material, the story said. The reporter's tone shifted, however, when he came across an old woman feeding a baby.

"One sweet little orphan ... was being fed from a bottle while lying upon the knees of a woman who had been one of the notorious Brooks' bush gang," he wrote. "The female thus occupied is low set, without the slightest trace of the milk of human kindness in her large and coarsely cut features, and it is a marvel to us that she takes such an interest in a helpless orphan. There is evidently some better part about her, which one fails to discover at first sight."

In 1904, after twenty-six years in the poorhouse, Jane Lewis, a.k.a. Jane Ward, died of "senile decay," as the registry put it, and was buried in the nearby pauper's grave. She was sixty-eight but listed as one hundred and one.

Acknowledgements

IN THE COURSE OF MY RESEARCH and writing, I received help from many people. Some are acknowledged in the text. I would like to cite others. Mary Jane McIntyre and Donald Luther, former chief justice of Newfoundland and Labrador, offered helpful suggestions on the manuscript. Marianne Ackerman in Prince Edward County, Anne Jane Grieve in Scarborough, and Craig Lapp in Montreal generously provided quiet rooms in which to write. I feel fortunate to have found Sean Marshall, a Toronto-based geographer and writer with an interest in Ontario heritage, to create the two maps. Stratford Perth Museum director John Kastner shared valuable information to help get me started on the book. Middlesex County archivist Chris Harrington helped me find not only Donald and Isabella McLeod's address but many other details as well. On research trips to Stratford, I usually stayed at the Albert Street Inn, now the Windsor Hotel, and always got a warm reception from Heather Schenck and Jodi Verellen. Thank you also to Richard Aniol, Carolynn Bart-Riedstra, Leslie Belland, October Browne, Gwyn Campbell, Suzanne Cook, Benjamin Dichter, Annie Finlay, Suzanne Jaeger, Peggy Krist, Donna Laframboise, Lucrezia LaRusso, Bob Moenck, Wanda Muszynski, Nora Jean Perkin, Tom Quiggin, Lutzen Riedstra, Marie Royer, Ellen Thomas, and Andre de Treville.

This is my third book with Dundurn Press. Thank you to Kirk Howard, Margaret Bryant, Kathryn Lane, Allison Hirst, and Elena Radic, and to copy editor Laurie Miller for his skilled and sensitive work. I am also grateful to the Ontario Arts Council for assisting with a fifteen hundred dollar Recommender Grant and a twelve hundred dollar Literary Creation Grant.

Bibliography

Ashenburg, Katherine. *Going to Town: Architectural Walking Tours in Southern Ontario*. Toronto: Macfarlane Walter & Ross, 1996.

Bale, Gordon. "Idington, John." In *Dictionary of Canadian Biography*, vol. 15, University of Toronto/Université Laval, 2003.

Beaumont, Ralph. *Cataract and the Forks of the Credit*. Erin, ON: The Boston Mills Press, 1973.

Bonnell, Jennifer L. *Reclaiming the Don: An Environmental History of Toronto's Don River Valley*. Toronto: University of Toronto Press, 2014.

Brode, Patrick. *Death in the Queen City: Clara Ford on Trial, 1895*. Toronto: Natural Heritage Books, 2005.

Brown, Ron. *Behind Bars: Inside Ontario's Heritage Gaols*. Toronto: Natural Heritage Books, 2006.

Cree, Janet Morton. *Ailsa Craig, Ontario, Canada: Centennial 1874–1974*. Ailsa Craig, ON: Ailsa Craig Centennial Committee, 1974.

Dubinsky, Karen. *Improper Advances: Rape and Heterosexual Conflict in Ontario, 1880–1929*. Chicago: University of Chicago Press, 1993.

Duke, Marion. *Where Town & Country Meet: Listowel Agricultural Society, 1856–2006, Celebrating 150 Years*. 2006.

Edwards, Peter. *Night Justice: The True Story of the Black Donnellys*. Toronto: Key Porter Books, 2004.

Fazakas, Ray. *The Donnelly Album: The Complete & Authentic Account of Canada's Famous Feuding Family*. Richmond Hill, ON: Firefly Books, 1995.

———. *In Search of the Donnellys*. Bloomington, Indiana: Trafford on Demand Publishing, 2001.

———. *In Search of the Donnellys: Revised Edition*. Bloomington, Indiana: Trafford on Demand Publishing, 2006.

———. *In Search of the Donnellys: Second Revised Edition*. Bloomington, Indiana: Trafford on Demand Publishing, 2012.

Feltes, Norman N. *This Side of Heaven: Determining the Donnelly Murders, 1880*. Toronto: University of Toronto Press, 1999.

Friedland, Martin L. *The Case of Valentine Shortis: A True Story of Crime and Politics in Canada*. Toronto: University of Toronto Press, 1986.

Guillet, Edwin Clarence. *The Mutilation of Jessie Keith: A Study of the Evidence in The Queen versus Almeda Chattelle, 1894–1895*. Vol. 28 of *Famous Canadian Trials*. [Toronto]: [Publisher not identified], 1945.

Hacking, Cyrus, and Beverley Bamford. *Listowel Ontario Past and Present: 1852–1921: Souvenir of Old Boys' and Girls' Reunion*. Listowel, ON: B.L.H. Bamford and G.C. Hacking, 1921.

Hucker, Jacqueline. "Decorative Mural Painting of Castle Kilbride." In *A National Soul: Canadian Mural Painting, 1860s–1930s*, by Marylin J. McKay. Montreal, Kingston, ON: McGill-Queen's University Press, 2002.

H.R. Page & Co. *Illustrated Historical Atlas of the County of Middlesex, Ontario*. Toronto: H.R. Page & Co., 1878.

Kelley, Thomas P. *The Black Donnellys: The True Story of Canada's Most Barbaric Feud*. Winnipeg: Harlequin Books, first edition, 1954. Toronto: Darling Terrace Publishing Co., thirty-second printing, 2016.

———. *Vengeance of the Black Donnellys: Canada's Most Feared Family Strikes Back from the Grave*. Winnipeg: Harlequin Books, first edition. 1962. Richmond Hill, ON: Firefly Books, 1995.

Leitch, Adelaide. *Floodtides of Fortune: The Story of Stratford and the Progress of the City Through Two Centuries*. Stratford, ON: The Beacon Herald Fine Printing Division, 1980.

McNichol, Vera. "Jessie Keith." In *Reveries of a Pioneer*. Kitchener, ON: Dixon Press, 1966.

Miller, Orlo. *Death to the Donnellys: A Novel*. Toronto: MacMillan of Canada, 1975.

———. *The Donnellys Must Die*. Toronto: MacMillan of Canada, 1962.

Murray, John Wilson. *Memoirs of a Great Detective: Incidents in the Life of John Wilson Murray*. London: William Heinemann, 1904.

Pfaff, Larry. *Historic St. Marys*. St. Marys, ON: St. Marys Journal Argus, 1995.

Phillips, Jim, and Joel Fortune. "Murray, John Wilson." In *Dictionary of Canadian Biography*, vol. 13, University of Toronto/Université Laval, 2003.

Reaney, James. *The Donnellys*. Toronto: Dundurn Press, 2008.

Stott, Glenn, and Greg Stott, eds. *Passing into Oblivion: The Diaries of William Porte, Lucan, Ontario, 1864–1898*. Anokra, ON: Anokra Press, 2009.

Wallace, W. Stewart. "The Murder of John Sheridan Hogan." In *Murders and Mysteries: A Canadian Series*. Toronto: Macmillan, 1931.

Waterston, Elizabeth. "Hogan, John Sheridan." In *Dictionary of Canadian Biography*, vol. 8, University of Toronto/Université Laval, 2003.

Wilson, Keith, and Melissa MacLean. *The Gallows and the Gaol: Crimes from the Perth and Waterloo County Jails*. Cambridge, ON: Lamplighter Books, 2003.

Image Credits

E. Jean Hodgins, private collection, published in *Older Pictures of Lucan Businesses and People in and Around Lucan*, Book 1: 145 (top)

John Goddard: 123, 124, 129, 131, 134, 135, 139, 144, 145 (bottom),147, 150 (top and bottom), 151, 152, 156, 158, 161, 167, 169, 172, 173, 205, 207, 210, 211, 214, 215, 218, 219, 220

Memoirs of a Great Detective, 1904: 59

Ray Fazakas: 148

Sean Marshall: 7, 22

St. Marys Museum and R. Lorne Eedy Archives: 8

Stratford-Perth Archives: 23 (top and bottom), 112, 196

Stratford-Perth Archives, Beacon Herald Subject Files, #2012.12: 202

Stratford-Perth Archives, Keith Family Collection, #2001.116.1: 11, 30

Stratford-Perth Archives, Keith Family fonds, #2001.116.1: 17, 29

Stratford-Perth Archives, Keith-Elliott Families, #2009.119.9: 32

Stratford-Perth Archives, Keith-Elliott Family fonds, #2009.119: 18, 116

Stratford-Perth Archives, People Photograph Collection: 73

Stratford-Perth Archives, People Photograph Collection, #1972.28.593(B): 55

Stratford-Perth Archives, People Photograph Collection, #1972.28.742: 175

Index